D0508534

Catching Rain

A woman rediscovers herself in
stories her lover has forgotten.

Sandi Paris

BALBOA.PRESS
A DIVISION OF HAY HOUSE

Balboa Press books may be ordered through booksellers or by contacting:

Balboa Press
A Division of Hay House
1663 Liberty Drive
Bloomington, IN 47403
www.balboapress.com
844-682-1282

Interior Image Credit: Dezerae Jobe Photography

Print information available on the last page.

ISBN: 979-8-7652-2624-7 (sc)
ISBN: 979-8-7652-2626-1 (hc)
ISBN: 979-8-7652-2625-4 (e)

Library of Congress Control Number: 2022904981

Balboa Press rev. date: 04/14/2022

Contents

This is for the exhausted and bewildered caregivers of the world. For courageous advocates who stand and speak for those without a voice. It is also a tribute to the brave hearts who open their minds and free one another to let fly the secrets that keep us all tethered. Finally, it is for the lovers who choose to stay and bear witness to the brutality of life. They will also be privileged to behold the luminous glow that shines through.

Prologue

MY LOVER HAS left me. There was no note propped on the coffee maker. He didn't storm out, slamming a door behind him. No other woman, or man, has lured him away. I am no less abandoned.

A sweet smile still warms the moment that Randy catches sight of me, but it does not glow with the heat of *knowing* like it did before. Before, is when we swam together in a river of words. Talking, sharing, never thinking it could run dry. Now, words are being erased from his brain and the stories they created are lost. Randy no longer knows *why* he smiles at this face and I am agonizingly unprepared for this kind of alone.

As I slowly lose this intelligent and beautiful man, who is losing himself, I begin to fear that the part of me changed by his love is also in danger of slipping away. The truckload of panic that has been parked in my chest since his diagnosis still revs its engine.

I have learned to calm myself by stretching fingers across a keyboard and feverishly pounding words into my computer. It is the way my feet pounded pavement years ago when I was a much younger woman who ran at dawn to escape a soulless first marriage. This time I am processing the unavoidable reality of a rare dementia, Frontotemporal Deterioration (FTD), that crept into my husband's brain sometime around his 50th birthday.

I am compelled to share my experiences of his illness but find that I must also describe who we are, what has been lost, and what is being found. Writing delivers a voice more lasting than a tongue. The ancient cave dweller who scratched pigment into stone walls is my brother, or sister.

Randy was my magic mirror. He showed me a woman much finer than I knew myself to be. His ears heard tender, foolish, and sometimes dark tales where he often identified humor and redemption I had missed. The sparkling blue eyes that reflected admiration, amusement, respect, and lust are now as foggy as the Northern California coast where we built our life together. When I get wound up about something, he can no longer suggest with his wry smile that I "might want to settle down now." I try to remind myself.

I must also remember not to expect gifts, or carefully selected cards with intimate messages. It has proven to be more difficult, impossible actually, to wrap myself up in long arms and describe the ways I am loved. I have short arms and self-doubt.

We all tell stories to make sense of our lives. Our own thoughts and words shape us as surely as those of other people. Randy would often admonish, "You should write that story down before you forget it." My response would be something like, "You will remember, youngster. Be sure to tell it to the grandkids." One brow would predictably raise itself over a stern blue eye to accent his reply, "I am not joking."

I also used to tease, like my friend Barbara, that I married a younger man so he could take care of me in my old age. The irony of this has not escaped me.

Before FTD, Randy was a 6'3" hunk of male tenderness and very human contradiction. He was strikingly attractive, intelligent, playful, often inappropriate, passionate, and wickedly sarcastic. An articulate speaker and skilled writer, Randy had a command of language. He was also a thoughtful and loving partner, largely because of what he learned from the women who came before me. I bow to each of them. Randy was a hands-on devoted father, who loved his son to a depth he had not known possible. A scientist and a thinker, insatiable reader and admitted news junkie, he was also an athlete who trained all winter for the summer season of 100-mile 'century' bicycle rides. He could be sophisticated if required and keenly witty when inspired.

Randy could also be ridiculously goofy, even before dementia made him more so. Sometimes forgetting his own height, he bumped his head on things that other people sailed under. His adult feet were the same size they have been since adolescence, but he would miscalculate and trip at unexpected times, bemoaning that "the world isn't built for people like me." When he blew his nose, he honked it like a circus clown's horn, startling everyone in the room and causing children to giggle with astonishment. He pretended not to notice. If we went out to eat, he took *forever* to order from a large menu because he had to consider every single option available. It was the same with other important decisions. Trying to hurry him up would slow him down. We could spend hours packing the car and preparing for a trip, but as soon as our seat belts clicked, Randy would open the car door again and say, "I'll be right back." We knew he was headed to the bathroom because there was something about the sound of a clicking seatbelt that worried his bowels.

Rarely taking himself too seriously, Randy was infamous for downgrading 'important' meetings by wearing silly hats topped with fish, eagles, or flamingos. He wore his uniform only when it was required for an official event of some sort. Until he became an administrator, he preferred the costume of a field biologist: Khaki cargo shorts with hiking boots, or sport sandals with white socks, even in the winter. He once selected bright red sandals (size 13) because they were on sale, and because he was red-green color blind. Whatever he saw when he looked at red, it pleased him.

Strolling in late – to everything – was a habit I came to terms with. An exception to this was on Feb 14th, Valentine's Day, when he arrived at the office early enough to place candy hearts and small paper valentines (the kind you buy in large bags) on staff and coworker's desks before they came to work. Later that evening, he would smile mischievously when describing a few people's confusion or stiff discomfort at such playfulness. He'd say, "I'd like to see those folks lighten up."

Randy had an open-door policy and encouraged his team to stop in for coffee or to snag candy from the 'feeding station' which was a large bowl that he kept on his desk. He reported that women overwhelmingly preferred chocolate. A scientific breakthrough. This was how he took the pulse of the office. He claimed to get as much valuable information during those walk-ins as in most formal meetings. Randy would use personal funds to purchase boxes of Ramones Bakery scones and fresh fruit for staff meetings. He wanted people to feel appreciated. He donated personal leave hours to co-workers who needed them, passed out $5 bills to panhandlers despite my objections, and alternated annual donations to organizations that we both supported. These included educational and environmental groups, along with the local women's refuge, homeless services, women's clinic, library, children's organizations, and the food bank. He would also help anybody who asked. If someone inquired how much he had given, he wouldn't know. He chose not to remember. This is who Randy was. He was playful, sometimes annoying, and one of the kindest and most generous people I've met in my life.

Randy did all the things medical experts now say we should do for brain health. Challenging his mind, he had advanced degrees, read incessantly, exercised daily, and aside from an occasional over-indulgence of IPA or sushi, he ate healthily. Randy had strong relationships and laughed repeatedly every day. Yet, his brain tissue is being ravaged.

So far, researchers have been unable to identify a cause. He has not inherited any of the currently identified genes that we might blame. This has forced me to accept that there may never be an answer to the uniquely human question of *Why? Why did this happen?*

Randy stopped asking that question when he no longer

understood it. I stopped asking when no one could provide a satisfactory answer. At some point, I remembered to ask myself that other question: *Why not?* Seriously. Why would any of us expect to be spared the random challenges or horrific tragedies that others experience? There are opportunities for ecstasy and agony. We often get both. It is the price of admission for full participation in an extraordinary and treacherous adventure called Life.

As I have moved through stages of disease with Randy, I have not needed words of reassurance. Legal counsel, long walks, friendship, and wine, yes. But not reassurance of the kind that most people offer. I cannot count the many occasions when caring people have felt compelled to say something that might help. I have heard things like, "God gave you to Randy because He knew that you were the only one who could handle this." Or "There is a reason for everything that happens." Or "Your life of repeated caregiving means that you still have a lesson to learn from a previous life." Each may be right. But what I know for sure is that these lovely people want to comfort me by offering something that comforts them.

For myself, I have become comfortable with ambiguity. I remind myself of two things: 1) Some things cannot be known; 2) Broken things cannot always be fixed. Whatever else I choose to believe at any given time, I find practical value and a measure of peace in these fundamental truths. I often allow myself to be titillated by not knowing what comes next. Even now.

After Randy's diagnosis, memories that once caused our souls to hum in harmony were tucked in the back of my mind for safe keeping. There was no time then for the deep wailing sorrow that would eventually break loose. I needed to focus on the looming threat of FTD and prepare for what was to come. Arming myself with as much information as I could gather, I rose off my knees to face the enemy and learned that it is impossible to fully prepare for something as unpredictable as this savage brain-sucking disease. Even as I have protectively wrapped him with love, catastrophic losses have mounted.

As Randy's personality changed, functional skills retreated and bizarre behaviors surfaced in their place. Sentimental novels and romanticized movies about the tragedy of dementia produce satisfying tears, but have not prepared me for the comedy or the financial havoc. Nor have they armed me for the day-to-day challenges I must work through. Information offered in medical literature is often too clinical or generalized to be useful. I couldn't conceive the depth of devastation; the inferno of anger; the cover-your-mouth disbelief; or the laugh-out-loud hilarity at some things I will describe. Losing our home and still-developing gardens did not cause my deepest anguish. Nor did it descend with our income when it plummeted, or when our dreams were shattered. I was bruised but unbroken when separated from our community of beautiful friends. Agony found me when words no longer had meaning and we could not touch each other with our stories.

The frontal and left-temporal lobes of Randy's brain are where neurons first began to shrivel and die. These areas are responsible for creating and processing language. Primary Progressive Aphasia (PPA) has accompanied the Semantic Variant of FTD, which is sometimes called Semantic Dementia. Now that he is mostly mute, the memory of his voice haunts me even more than the memory of his touch.

I ache to hear Randy's sharp and timely wit and am impatient for his thoughtful, intelligent, perspective. He needs to try again to explain fish and football to me, and why each is important to the world. I want him to keep explaining to science-resistant people why we cannot continue doing things the way we used to. Randy was prone to passionate and sometimes outrageous political rants which I enjoyed monitoring and often took part in. I miss being repeatedly surprised by the quality of his singing voice whenever he joined in with Dave Mathews, Don Henley, or Eric Clapton while traveling in the car. I do not miss the pounding rock music that would briefly vibrate through the neighborhood when he and his son, Jordan, set off for a weekend of snowboarding together. He explained through the lowered truck window, while both heads bobbed up and down to the beat, that this was how they "got pumped to conquer the mountain." Even his sexually playful and inappropriate comments have become desperately endearing. I want to giggle or chastise him for them again. Most of all, I miss hearing him chant "Sandi Girl!" as he enticed me in from the garden by holding a glass of wine over the deck railing so that I would dramatically throw down rakes or shovels to run up and save it from falling. We laughed every single time.

Randy would mischievously taunt me with "Sandi Girl" so I could scold and remind him I am a woman, not a girl. He preferred women. After FTD, all females became 'girls' regardless of age, but I was comforted knowing that it was not due to a willful brain dysfunction.

While I delight in the strange little chuckle Randy makes now, I miss the guffaw of a laugh that would erupt when something surprised or delighted him. We both recognized the comedy of life and even saw it through tears shed over unexpected tragedy. The frail arrogance of our species led us to laugh at ourselves and I remember howling together during a live show, when wonderfully profane George Carlin warned us that the earth will shake us off like a bad case of the fleas. As this is becoming more likely, I am no longer laughing. I want Randy to console me with words of hope he can no longer provide.

I now communicate with hands that point, wave, and touch. My face exaggerates expressions, looks surprised, grimaces, or grins with delight, just for him. My tone of voice stimulates or soothes him with rhyming sounds and songs. To everyone else, I appear to have my own neurological challenges.

I have begun to recognize the sweetness in these quieter

times, but never forget that precious words were the tools that allowed us to describe to each other our feelings and experiences, and to articulate our reasons for loving. Words asked questions and told of hurt, disappointment, or anger. They allowed us to share fears and dreams, to problem-solve, negotiate, challenge, cheer, console, and entertain one another. We read words to each other in bed at night and left voice messages every day. And we shared our most closely guarded secrets, sometimes with head-bowing shame. The magic of language allowed Randy and I to create a profound intimacy. I sometimes surf a crushing wave of longing for the sound of his voice whispering again, "I do love you, Sandi Girl."

Several years into our journey with dementia, stories from the past began to rise like a gathering of ghosts. They kindly lifted my head to keep me from drowning. I have accepted that Randy no longer comprehends my words yet often feel as though my next breath won't come until I tell him things he used to know. I don't do it for him. I do it so I can breathe.

These events don't present themselves in chronological order, but randomly resurrect during ordinary moments like a walk, holiday, place, photograph, flower, movie, or song. I let them escort me back and forth between moments of now and stories of then, the time before dementia. I know that one day the events of my life will escape my own memory and float off somewhere to mix with all the other stories that have ever been told.

In the meantime, I have rediscovered the uneasy peace in surrender by walking with this wretched disease. It is FTD that holds me in the present where new stories are being created. These sprout like supple vines to wrap around old woody tales of the past. Those who advise us to "never look back" are afraid of getting stuck there with old regrets, trauma, and grief we left behind. I am not afraid. I allow the past to step in for a visit when

I want to be reminded of where I've been; what I've learned; and who I've loved along the way.

Some people may be uncomfortable with graphic details provided. I don't believe that life becomes more sacred by hiding distasteful moments. Exposing and examining what is not pretty allows us to feel less alone in our humanness and imperfection. Randy and I examined the dark crevices of life together and I will not abandon that practice now.

I invite readers to cry and laugh with me, even as dementia drags Randy closer to the abyss. Perhaps they will feel more informed or less afraid. I would like that.

I now imagine Randy's brain as something like a sponge that is slowly being squeezed dry. Everything he understood about the world and his place in it, all the things he once knew about me and other people he loved, are falling like rain. Drop by precious drop, story by precious story. When I capture them, they fill my mind like gusts of wind blowing into the sails of a floundering ship. As I tell them to Randy again, they set me back on course and I am fearless once more.

Note from Author

My intent is to tell the truth of what I have experienced, observed, or been told, while also recognizing that memory is capricious and undependable. These are my memories, not Randy's and certainly not anyone else's. I will share some things Randy told me but leave most of his own stories with him. They are not mine to tell.

Some individuals described are a deliberate mix of more than one type of person, as are some events, dates, and locations. Names, genders, and other identifiable traits have been omitted or changed to protect privacy where appropriate.

I must warn that there are a few profane words I am known to utter on occasion. It seems important to be authentic here, where I expose my many flaws and tell of uncomfortable things. The most appalling words are direct quotes from someone else's mouth. These are included to demonstrate how they were used to burn racist ideas and bigoted values into young minds. These words are not allowed to ride on my otherwise unpredictable tongue.

I

The Ever-Present Past

Our past often chases us into the future

Hold On

I HAVE PULLED to the side of the road because I can't see. When I left your memory care facility just a few minutes ago, the wind was picking up and clouds were dark and heavy. Now they have emptied themselves in a powerful deluge that pummels my windshield. It feels personal. The reason I can't see is not only because of the rain but because Dylan's song "Make You Feel My Love" is also playing on the radio. The lyrics have slammed into my chest and I imagine fighting my way back through the storm to claw away the cobwebs that cloud your eyes and prevent me from knowing whether you feel loved. Six years after your dementia diagnosis, tears stream down my face again.

I cried then — in front of the team of specialists at the study center in San Francisco. They delivered their final verdict while facing us as we sat together at one end of an impressive conference table with a strategically placed box of tissue. It was the culmination of intense medical and neuropsychological testing, imaging, and other evaluations over a period of months. As they talked, my brain began to buzz like a bag of bees. When I could form a clear thought it was, *"Why can't it be a tumor?"* Tumors are often treatable.

By nature, I am an intuitive, fly-by-the-seat-of-the-pants kind of person. It was necessary to train my adult self to be an organized and efficient planner. I do not plan because it ensures a predictable outcome but because it gives me a false sense of control, which I understand is a comforting myth. When I have a big decision to make, I imagine the worst possible things that could happen so I can prepare for them. Some people make a living by telling other people to plan for success, rather than failure. I ditched those seminars. For me, planning for failure is like filling an emergency earthquake kit. Once I have a backup plan, I can relax and get on with enjoying the risks of life. This is my personal dance with the universe and I often hear its laughter.

So, there I was, caught with no plan because, unlike an earthquake, dementia at age 50 was unimaginable.

I remember watching you smile and nod with steady eye contact during the explanations from each of the professionals as they detailed what their tests had revealed. If they were anyone else, sitting anywhere else, they would have believed that you thoroughly understood what they were saying. But these people had seen the inside of your brain. They knew that the areas responsible for processing and producing language were compromised, along with the areas that regulate emotion, judgement, and behavior. When they finished talking, you looked over at me and laughed out loud, pointing at the tears running down my cheeks. You seemed delighted, asking, "Why are those?" Then you looked across the table and explained to the team, "She is an older girl" as if to clear up questions they might have about those tears, which you couldn't name. We all laughed with you. It was damn funny. And it felt good to laugh in the face of such terrifying news.

Now you rarely speak. When you do, it is just a couple of short, two-word, phrases that seem to feel good on your tongue. You no longer produce tears of your own while I am filled to the brim with both. Spontaneous words and uninvited tears spill over at unexpected times, often in public places like restaurants or grocery stores. Usually after someone asks how things are going.

At night, when I can't sleep, grief and memories slop around in my skull like a bucket of mud. I drain the tears that puddle on top by pounding my pillow, like punching holes in Hoover Dam. Gentler with the slurry of words that remain, I empty these into my laptop, so they don't get lost again. I want to remember everything.

Today, when I left you sitting on the couch at your facility, I stopped at the door to wave goodbye and called out "Later Gator," as usual. You chuckled and responded, "Hold on!" This wasn't because you had an opinion about my leaving. "Hold on!" is one of those phrases like, "Oh, wow!" that you say when you do speak. Friends and family have also begun to say, "Hold on!" We are amused at how often it fits. *Hold on! Here comes life!*

I don't know exactly when I started reintroducing myself, and yourself, to you. It was intermittent and unauthorized like deterioration of your brain cells. In early stages of disease, you would look to me for help understanding a question or retrieving lost words so that you could communicate without too much frustration. As you gradually talked less, I talked more, filling what seemed to be empty space. I would talk you through the steps of your day and provide names of people and things you could no longer retrieve. This was when some words still had meaning. As they became just sounds, you would still watch my face and listen like you enjoyed the background music of my voice. But now there has been another change that I missed, while I was talking.

Just a few days ago, after rubbing lotion into the dry skin on your feet and legs, I was cheerfully chatting away as I put your slippers back on. You abruptly stood up and firmly took my hand in yours, then led me to the door. You did this in the same quietly deliberate way that you do when you want me to walk the hall with you. This time you gently pushed me through the door ahead of you, then turned back into your room and shut it behind you. I found myself standing alone in the hallway, smiling and shaking my head. I hadn't noticed my words becoming a burden. An expectation you couldn't meet. We have all been swarming about, buzzing with words, while the things that you understand and respond to are the touch of a hand, the taste of a cookie, and

3

the smiles on our faces. You also understand laughter which has connected us every single day. A family member once said, with grave disapproval, "You are so disrespectful when you laugh at Randy." I considered this for a moment, trying to understand his perspective, but then I dissolved into more laughter. Appearances are less important now, nor have they ever had much to do with actual dignity or respect. Moments of laughter are precious and I cannot imagine stifling them because your dementia behavior is uncomfortable for others. When we look away, or respond with sadness or disapproval, we miss an opportunity to connect. You may not understand what words mean but you understand tone and attitude. Laughter still sounds and feels good to you and you usually respond in kind, with smiles and chuckles. You do not respond with smiles when someone is frustrated or embarrassed for you.

The rain slows and the song ends but I remain parked on the side of the road. I cannot drive home until my tears have also slowed. When I finally walk through the door of my cozy little house where you have never lived, you somehow feel present. I forgot to leave the radio on and it is hauntingly quiet until our manly Yorkshire terrier, Gus-Gus, wakes up to perform his greeting dance. The sound of his joyful barking and nails tapping on the hardwood floor chases the gloom away. I pick him up and rub his ears before pouring red wine into a small coffee mug on the counter, where it has been waiting for the coffee it didn't receive this morning. Gus snuggles onto my lap as I sit down and wrap my hands around the mug. His gaze is adoring, and I feel like I can trust my world for one lovely moment. I sip slowly and think of how ridiculous it would be for me to continue flooding you with words that you cannot process. I am not even sure you remember who I am or my significance in your life. You smile and seem to recognize me, but I know that you may just be welcoming a friendly face with a happy voice and a cookie.

4

I force myself to acknowledge that whatever images you still hold in your mind, they are no longer painted with words. It is when I sit with you in silence that you now seem to absorb my presence. Silence has become more intimate than talking. If I can remain quiet long enough, you sometimes put your arm around my shoulders or reach over and lace your fingers with mine. You will glance sideways at me without turning your head. If I lock eyes with you, I swear it is a smile of satisfaction that creeps onto your face.

Words are not what you need now. They are what I need. I vow to limit the time that I talk out loud to you. Instead, I will fill my quiet evenings talking to you on my computer. This is how I will *hold on*.

Tomorrow when I visit, I will say, "I am remembering how I met Mary in the old graveyard behind St. Mary's church." You won't understand those words but may grin and say, "Hold on" or "Oh, wow." Then again, you may not respond at all. I will sit with you and rub your feet, maybe help you with lunch, or put in a music video for you to watch and sway to. I might push a ball through the air toward you and encourage you to toss it back. You now prefer to hand it to me rather than throw it, but you instinctively catch it over and over, regardless of which angle or speed it approaches. Your motor skills are intact. When you tire of catching the ball, you will keep it. Setting it down next to you and avoiding my eyes, you will sever our connection like hanging up a telephone. When I get ready to leave, I will bend down in front of you and bring my face close to yours so I can look directly into your eyes. You will smile again. This smile is always more tender than the others. Perhaps you understand I will soon leave you in peace. I always whisper, "I love you, Randy Man. You are the best man I know." When I kiss your cheek, you often try to kiss me on the mouth. You have mossy teeth now, but I never turn away. I will wave from the doorway again. You won't wave back because waving is something you no longer do. I begin to think about Mary...

Your office on the Northern California coast was located in a historic school building that could no longer meet earthquake and other safety standards for children. They converted the building into professional offices which were then leased to the agency you worked for. If a group of adult scientists could not escape an earthquake, there are some political or religious groups who might construe this to be a divine form of natural selection.

Across the street was a tiny turn-of-the century church that still wore her virginal white paint with pride. It's double doors once opened wide to welcome people of that small community. The tall steeple no longer housed the big Brass bell that once beckoned them by ringing out from the hillside and down over the town. It could have been an illustration in a child's storybook.

The old church had been closed to services for many years which allowed the silent steeple to become home to a pair of beautiful white-faced barn owls. You introduced me to them one evening when I picked you up for dinner after you had worked late. Every night around dusk, at some secret signal known only to them, they would emerge from their nest inside the bell tower and open their large ghostly wings against the darkening sky to glide out and begin their nightly hunt for mice in the fields close by. Their wings made no detectible sound and it was a hauntingly lovely thing to watch.

On an unusually warm summer evening with soft golden light, I decided to set up my tripod and attempt to capture the moment the owls took flight. I got there in plenty of time to select the perfect spot and put everything in place, with the steeple silhouetted against the western sky. Watching the sun slide toward the dunes of the Pacific Ocean in the distance, there was no fog and a few light clouds showed some soft color. It looked like I might also catch a beautiful sunset.

The town was beginning to quiet as vehicles were parked for the night when a loud voice suddenly rose from the cemetery behind the church. I walked softly down the side of the building toward the rear to cautiously peer around the corner. While gravestones testified to the temporary nature of life, it was the noisy contribution of a very-much-alive elderly woman that drew my attention. She was standing alone in front of a simple stone and appeared to be both round and tiny, with a slightly humped back. Her short grey hair was damp and she was dressed in a pink sweatsuit with white tennis shoes. A brown fanny pack was buckled around her waist with the pocket in front, across her soft belly. She was holding an old-fashioned wooden cane in one hand, which she alternately tapped on the stone or gestured with, waving it around in the air as she laughed and talked boisterously to that grave.

I turned to sneak away, but she caught my movement and brightly called out, "Hello there!" Feeling like an intruder, I apologized for bothering her. She snorted, "This is a public place. Is it not?" It felt like permission, so I moved closer to introduce myself. She nodded her head in response and said, "I'm Mary." Mary told me she just came from the community pool next door where she "lubricated her old bones" by swimming. After swimming, she often stopped by to tell her husband, George, about her day while waiting for her ride home.

As Mary cheerfully shared that George had died a few years before, my somber nod led her to arcuately read my mind. She snorted again before clarifying that she certainly knew his ears couldn't hear her anymore but thought his spirit might. "I used to talk to George silently in my mind, but it wasn't the same. I decided you all can tolerate this daffy old woman!" Her laugh was shrill before she became more serious and quietly confided, "I don't feel so lonely when I talk out-loud to George."

When Mary's taxi arrived, I gave her a hug and told her that I hoped I could be as joyful as she was after such a sad loss. She pointed an arthritic finger at me and responded sternly, "We should never allow sorrow to push joy away!" Waving through the window as the taxi drove off, Mary left me to consider how feelings of joy and sorrow might dance together if we give them permission. Just like the past and present.

I got back to my camera in time to see the owls taking flight. I missed my shot and caught the far-off glow of a sunset that I had also missed. Several years later the old church burned down, reportedly from the fire of homeless 'travelers' trying to stay warm on a cold foggy night. They may have believed they would be welcomed by taking refuge in such a holy place. I did not attempt to weigh physical or spiritual comfort against the material and historical loss of that brutal exchange. I would never see the owls or Mary again.

It is reassuring to remember how interrupted plans so often lead to serendipitous moments like that. I had pushed my encounter with Mary to the back of my mind, along with other memories that are still waiting to rise and offer fresh perspective when most needed.

Like Mary, I feel less lonely when I talk directly to you. I think she would be glad to know that I have not allowed the sorrow of your illness to push away the joy of life. Sorrow gracefully slides back for Joy when she kicks up her heels in a field of wildflowers after a wet spring. Or when Gus-Gus bounces around, wanting to play. It is joyous gratitude that still surges through my nostrils with smells of the forest when I walk under the trees. I feel jubilant each time I see a wild animal that is thriving, despite our self-serving disregard. Like pollinators and browsers, I am enticed by gardens that are full and untidy, overflowing with colorful distraction and hidden secrets of understory. I am still filled with wonder when contemplating art, or the magic of children. Most surprising, my heart continues to swell with pleasure when my body insists on stomping to a musical beat or swaying to a melody. I remember how you would grin and dance with long arms stretched out in wild abandon until other dancers dodged and ducked. Now, when I celebrate your demented little smile, both Sorrow and Joy come to dance with me.

Even though you are sleeping across town and cannot hear me, I read out loud what I have written. I pretend you are lying next to me, listening, and can almost feel your icy feet as you wrap your giant legs and arms around me to get warm, spooning and nuzzling the back of my neck and falling asleep that way. I can hear you snore your soft purr...

Anything but That

IT IS MY son's birthday. He considers this to be equivalent to a national holiday and we celebrate accordingly. Unlike Scott, you are no longer aware of birthdays or the pleasure in celebrating them. Scott hasn't seen you for several years, but he misses you. I know this because the other day, we were washing our camper van while streaming music from my cell phone, when your voice suddenly blasted through the speakers, "Hey Sandi. How's it going?" It was an old message from two phones ago that was somehow transferred into a music file. Scott hadn't heard your voice since that terrible weekend three years ago when I realized that your brain had abandoned him, too. After that, I kept him away from you and he eventually stopped asking where you were. I began to wonder if he had forgotten, but when your voice rang through the speakers, Scott immediately recognized it. He thought you were calling at that very moment and tried to answer, saying, "Randy! I'm coming, Randy!" His stubby legs struggled to climb up into the van as he frantically reached for the phone. Not only did he recognize your voice, but he was very excited to hear it. His huge forgiving heart immediately expanded to welcome you back, even after being gone for so long. Catching him before he got all the way into the van, I wrapped Scott in a big hug and explained that it was a very old message and you weren't talking on the phone. He listened closely as I reminded him you were still living in a 'hospital' because your brain was broken and wouldn't let you talk anymore. There was no response for a long while and then he said, "Oh." As he walked over to pick up the towel he had been using to dry the car, a wave of love nearly knocked me over. He does that to me. I encouraged him to be sad if he wanted to. He didn't. Scott's love is as uncomplicated as his acceptance of life. There are no strings. Besides, I promised pizza for dinner when we finished washing the van.

I begin to think about the time when I first realized I needed to protect Scott from you. It was something I could never have anticipated.

You stood calmly, waiting for me to uncouple a shopping cart from one of the long trains that are docked at the entrance to Costco. Standing 6 feet, 3 inches tall, you were wearing khaki shorts and a black T-shirt that my brother had given you. It displayed the colorful image of a Chinook salmon on the front and I remember a young couple laughing when they read the message printed under the salmon: "Spawn until you die!"

As a biologist, you honored all forms of reproduction. You had previously enjoyed reactions to this shirt, but now ignored their laughter as if it had no connection to you. They, in turn, had no way of recognizing this subtle indication that something was terribly wrong.

We moved into the store and your body suddenly stiffened, freezing in mid-stride like someone had pushed 'pause' on a remote. I followed your gaze across the warehouse to see that it was locked on a young man with Down syndrome. You began pointing toward him and shouting in alarm. "LOOK! That guy is MESSED UP." When you started pulling me in his direction, I understood that you wanted us to get as close as possible so you could be sure that I saw what you saw. I also knew you might continue to shout, point, and follow the boy through the store if I couldn't redirect you. I tried physically holding you back while responding in a reassuring tone. "That's a NICE Guy. He's like our Scooter." When you showed no sign of stopping, I rushed to push my cart across the aisle to block you. You moved me and the cart out of your way and I knew it was time to deploy serious deterrents. I grabbed a huge Costco-sized bag of potato chips that were on display and waved them in your face. "Look... Look..."

You had clearly forgotten what you once knew about Down syndrome, but you had not forgotten how utterly delicious potato chips taste. After I opened the bag and watched you blissfully surrender to their salty crunch, I swallowed the bitterness that crawled up my own throat.

The boy and his family moved safely out of view, unaware of the little scrimmage that had just taken place. This time, I did not have to pull the 'business card' from my pocket, which I usually offered during an 'event.' The card says: "Please excuse my companion's language or behavior. It is caused by a form of dementia, FTD, that is like Alzheimer's Disease." People frequently tossed them on the floor and occasionally in my face because I offered them at the precise moment that your victims were attempting to escape. They did not invite this into their lives. I understood.

You received your diagnosis three years prior to this incident. Since then, you lost your job; could no longer ride your beloved bicycle; or drive your adventure-seeking truck. You still functioned well in other ways and seemed to recognize most family and friends. It was not always clear when a piece of useful knowledge had completed the process of vacating your brain.

You once knew how an extra chromosome could mistakenly be produced and then duplicated in every cell of a developing fetus, splitting, and multiplying over and over, until eventually becoming an infant with Down syndrome. Now you didn't. You no longer understood this inseparable piece of my son's identity and I had ignored important clues.

When Scott visited a few weeks prior to this incident, you had refused to engage him. Rather than the usual bear hug, you greeted him with a look of detached confusion. I distracted Scott and told myself that it was just a mood. I did this even after you became unmistakably upset when he teased you in the same way that you had teased each other for years. Scott called "Look!" while pointing away from the table and stealing a bite of food off your plate. There was no exaggerated dismay or playful retaliation from you. Instead of laughter, he received a silent and suspicious frown. You refused to share the big TV so he could play Wii Bowling. There was no invitation to walk up to the mailbox together, or to creep outside at dusk and call "ErrrReet, ErrrReet," to excite the Chorus frogs who lived in our pond. You didn't want to play checkers with him. Then, when Scott grabbed your wallet off the table and ran giggling to hide it, you did not chase him in fun like you used to. You were upset and roared, "WHY DID HE DO THAT?"

Scott's face turned ashen and he backed away, avoiding eye contact. He grew very quiet and stayed uncomfortably close to me for the rest of that weekend. He began watching you warily while rocking back and forth between his two feet, a sure sign of distress. I reassured him he had done nothing wrong and explained that "your brain was sick and not working right." Whatever Scott understood about that explanation, it didn't change what he felt. You didn't love him anymore.

It was in Costco where I was made to understand that an essential piece of myself had also vacated your memory. Scott's story is a chapter from my story and woven into the fabric of our relationship. How you responded the first time I told it to you was one reason I loved you.

As I absorbed the reality of this new loss, a vivid image filled my mind. Standing in that warehouse, I imagined thousands of colorful words and familiar faces pouring out of your open hinged mouth like a giant puppet vomiting confetti. They spewed across the concrete floor to pile up around my feet and I began to unravel.

The anguish I felt was not unlike the day Scott was born. This wasn't what I had planned, and you were no longer the person I had chosen to wrap my life around. While I celebrated every milestone Scott reached, each day with you was now measured in loss. You were devolving into a self-centered child who was 6'3" tall and difficult to control. FTD had replaced your thoughtful qualities with an impulsive and random goofiness. You were beginning to need physical care and protection. Your keen intelligence was gone, along with your deep sense of compassion and empathy. You no longer seemed to feel *love*.

Feelings of love do not originate in the heart, but in the brain. It seems especially cruel to erase this essence of humanity while a heart is still beating. I began to grieve like a widow without a body to bury.

Over the next few days, I cradled Scott's story in my mind and eventually began writing it down. Resurrecting words and images we had shared those many years ago, I discovered that I was also resurrecting you... the man I had fallen in love with. When I began to tell this story again, I could see your clear blue eyes narrow and widen at all the right times. Witnessing your tears well up, I also saw your head shake back and forth in disbelief again. Your lips on my forehead felt warm and your long fingers laced with mine felt firm. I was impressed once more that you had researched the syndrome that shaped my son's mind and body so you could better understand. Your admiring smile when you called me "courageous" came back to me like a shot of brandy on a cold night and I felt it moving through my veins again.

As a young woman, I had tripped, crawled, and stumbled toward the courage and strength that you so thoroughly embraced. I am recharged by imagining you sitting next to me again, listening to this story that you used to know:

The world has changed since 1967, when I was 21 years old and expecting my first child. My first husband was in the army and had spent a year on the border of Thailand and Vietnam, flying supplies into the war zone. When he returned, I quit my job in San Francisco to join him on a training base in Fort Smith, Arkansas and soon became pregnant. We looked forward to returning to California after discharge, which would be a few months after the baby was born.

One morning, my German friend, Dagmar, who was also a military wife, was visiting. Holding a cup of coffee, she gazed down from our upstairs window toward a boarded-up old building in the field below. We lived on the edge of town in a one-bedroom apartment built over a garage. A deer had been browsing there just a few moments earlier. Suddenly she called me over to point out a young man, not a deer. He was stocky with an awkward, flat-footed gait, and his tongue protruded from a slightly gaping mouth. As we watched him, I realized he had features I was familiar with.

I was 9 years old when I noticed a strange girl next door to the house that my family was moving into. She was standing in her yard, watching us through the wire fence. Her head was tilted to one side and her tongue protruded from her mouth. Her eyes were shaped like almonds, she had short arms and legs, and her words were difficult for me to understand. I asked my mother, "What's wrong with that girl?" She explained that she was a "Mongoloid." Not a child with a condition, but a condition that was tossed over the child like a hooded cloak on Halloween, hiding everything else that she also was. My next question, "What made her that way?" was answered with, "Only God knows." The conversation was firmly terminated when she said, "There, but for the grace of God, go you." I remember feeling grateful that God had graced me by not making me like her but was left to wonder what the little girl had done to upset Him. That was my first exposure to Down syndrome.

As we watched the young man below us, I saw he was clean and neat. Someone cared about him. He began walking slowly around the old structure with a focus, studying each window with his head tilted to one side. When he picked up a piece of metal from the ground and began to pry off the wood covering a window, it appeared a criminal act was about to take place. My friend grabbed the telephone to dial the police. I took it from her saying, "Maybe we should try talking to him first."

She warned, "he could be dangerous," and then added more gently, "he is retarded and he could get hurt." She reached for the phone again and dialed. As she explained to the dispatcher what was happening and described the suspect, I could hear a man's voice on the other end. The dispatcher said, "Oh, that's Tommy. I'll have an officer come by and pick him up. He lives with his grandma a few blocks over and slips out for a little adventure once in a while. Thanks for calling."

After just a few minutes, a patrol car leisurely maneuvered through tall grass toward the old building. Tommy stood watching it approach and then calmly walked over and got into the front seat. It was clearly not his first ride in a police car. The gentle policing touched me and there was no burning question in my mind about why it was so rare to see people like Tommy in our communities. Dust swirled behind as we watched them drive away. I rubbed my 6-month pregnant belly and commented, "I could handle anything but that." Dagmar nodded in somber agreement.

Two months later, I woke to find four men standing at the foot of my hospital bed. Through my medication-induced fog, I thought they might be angels. Unlike the beautiful female angels from Sunday school stories, they did not open their arms with reassuring smiles. These man-angels stood like security guards and I did not feel reassured. As I struggled to focus, I realized that one was my husband. His skin was grey and his red eyes looked less like an angel and more like a zombie who'd been out all night. He seemed helpless, yet somehow dangerous, all at the same time. I was to become very familiar with this confusing trait.

It became apparent that I was neither dead nor dreaming

when the fuzzy image of a tiny little baby crawled into my mind. I remembered where I was and that they had refused to let me hold the baby. All the other mothers on my floor, including my roommate, Debbie, had been holding and feeding their babies on a regular schedule. I asked the nurses when they would bring my baby to me and they always looked away before saying, "You need to get stronger" or "The doctor will talk to you soon." They would then give me a little white pill called "Doctor's Orders" and I would take another nap.

Two nights before the angel lineup, I had climbed out of bed and shuffled past the empty nurse's station to the big window around the corner, where babies were proudly displayed for family and friends to fawn over. This was back in the days when we still believed gender was set in the stone of a birth certificate. We wrapped baby girls in pink blankets, and boys were wrapped in blue. They printed the family name on a tag attached to the bassinet so it could be seen from the hallway through the window. I navigated back and forth in front of that window several times, thinking each beautiful baby looked like it could be mine. I searched the name tags on every blue baby but could not find our name. I checked all the pink babies in case he was accidently wrapped in the wrong color, but our name was not there either. I checked every single pink and blue baby one more time in case they had misspelled our name. None supported that possibility. Each baby had someone else's name and I started to panic until I noticed a little blue bundle all alone in the back of the nursery. I tapped on the window so the lady tending to the infants would look up. I pointed to the bundle in the back and showed her my wrist band through the glass. Her expression reflected panic as she shook her head 'no' and picked up a wall phone. Moments later a 6-foot-tall woman with huge shoulders and hands, came speeding around the corner from the nurses'station, demanding to know what I was doing there. When she escorted me back to my room, saying that I had "defied doctor's orders," I recognized the old familiar burn of rebellion beginning to smolder in my empty belly, until she gave me the little white pill.

The next night, I crept down the hall again and ducked into a bathroom near the nurses' station until I could be sure the coast was clear. When I got to the window, a different woman was taking care of the babies and I tapped again. This time, when I showed her my wrist band and pointed to the blue bundle that was still in the back, she moved the bassinet forward so I could see him.

My tiny 5 1/2-pound child looked like he had been thrown out of a moving vehicle, which I suppose he had when he was ejected from my pulsing body. His wildly misshapen little head was splotched with blood blisters and his eyes were still swollen nearly shut. Both sides of his face had dark purple bruises from the forceps that were used to facilitate his transition into the unforgiving light of that delivery room. I later learned forceps were necessary because of the medications I was given to induce what they called a "Twilight Sleep" which dulled the pain of childbirth. They no longer give these medications for several reasons, one being that they slow, thus extend labor, which is not good for babies. In my case they also caused me to crawl over the rails of the bed because I thought I had to go to the bathroom when I was actually close to delivery.

As I looked at this poor beat-up little baby, a hand flew up to cover my mouth. The horror I felt was evident on my face because the attendant quickly returned the bassinet to the back, separating him from the others again. I got back to my room just before the big nurse came roaring and scolding. This time she gave me two little pills. That is the last thing I remembered before the man-angel lineup.

My husband remained with the men at the foot of my bed. He would glance at me from time to time but didn't maintain eye contact. He did not come to my side and hold my hand, like in the movies. A good soldier, he kept his eyes focused on the doctor in charge. After a silence that seemed to last hours, this man cleared his throat and announced: "Your baby is *not* alright!"

His words bounced around my head without making much sense. My son didn't look like the Gerber Baby, but I had counted 10 tiny fingers and 10 little toes, and I'd heard him cry. Well actually he croaked, sounding like an adorable little frog. Before they whisked him away, I could see that he was breathing and making noise which assured me, in my medicated stupor, that he was just fine.

As I tried to absorb this new information, I looked at his father again. His pain was palpable, but he couldn't share it with me. His eyes began to move between the Doctor and the door, like he was hoping to be excused. I would one day comply.

The Doctor stridently explained that the baby was "profoundly retarded" because he was "Mongoloid" (a term other medical professionals no longer used) and had also suffered oxygen deprivation during the long labor and delivery. He neglected to mention the drugs that had also entered the baby's system. This doctor drilled in his message of doom, saying my baby had a hole in his heart that is "life threatening" and "even if he lives, he is so brain damaged you will need to set an alarm clock for his feeding because he won't know enough to cry when he's hungry."

I asked, "Is he going to die?" The doctor replied, "It would be a blessing." My flame of rebellion flickered out. If there was nothing that could be done for my baby, then I would not have to figure out what to do. I imagined him painlessly slipping away in a deep peaceful sleep, solving this terrible problem for all of us. Besides, this wasn't the baby I had dreamed of and bought adorable clothes and toys for. I had no idea what to do with this poor little retarded baby.

They recommended that we immediately relinquish parental rights, giving him a priority spot for institutional care. During the 1960's, this was still standard procedure in some states, including Arkansas. He would go into foster care for six months and then into an institution for a lifetime. The doctor began to soothe us with certainty, "This child will never know the difference and you can go on to have normal children." He then frightened us by promising it would be the "biggest mistake of your lives" to take this baby home. If we did and later found we couldn't manage, "there would be a five-year waiting period for placement." He forecast guilt, saying it would be unfair to raise him with other children, as "he will consume all of your attention and resources." The Doctor finally became very fatherly and for the first time in my life, I felt relieved that someone was telling me what to do. He patted my hand and said the papers would be drawn up for us to sign the next morning. It was only when they turned their backs to leave that I began to comprehend the enormity of what was occurring. My baby would not be coming home with me. He might die. If he didn't die, he would be condemned to life in an institution located in another state, far away from where we would be living.

They moved me to a private room so I didn't disturb others with my sobbing. They would still not allow me to hold the baby, saying it was "for the best."

At around 1:30 AM, I was lying wide-awake despite the little white pills, when a young man walked into my darkened room and pulled a chair up next to my bed. Through swollen eyelids, I recognized him as a doctor from the previous morning's line-up.

He explained that he was doing a temporary residency in Arkansas and would soon return to California. He read in my chart that we would also return to California after my husband was discharged from the army and asked if this was correct. I nodded 'yes.'

This young doctor asked if I was aware there were "services" in California that are not available in Arkansas. I had no idea what he was talking about. He explained, "In California there is community support and special programs for anyone challenged by a developmental disability like Down syndrome." He told me these services took place in the "least restrictive environment possible, and rarely included institutional care." I'd never heard this language before. He reported that with this support, most families in California raised their own Down syndrome babies and these children were often happy and loving additions to their communities where they attended school and held jobs. This young doctor was the first person to suggest that my baby had been affected by the medications I was given before delivery. He also told me that heart murmurs caused by blood pumping through little holes in the heart, sometimes closed spontaneously or were surgically repaired. He noted the baby was already more responsive as the medications cleared his little body and he felt confident that my son was "not a vegetable" but could have a rich and full life. Finally, he gently said, "We all deserve an opportunity to try." I felt my shoulders square and my head rise like a soldier preparing for battle.

We heard nurses transporting hungry babies through the halls and past my door to other mothers for the 2 AM feeding. The young doctor looked at me and asked, "Would you like to feed your baby?" I nodded 'yes.' He stood up and stepped into the hallway, stopping a nurse who was returning with empty arms from a neighboring room. He gestured toward me and asked her to please bring my baby to me. She looked confused and responded stiffly that "THE doctor gave orders that she is not to have her baby."

The intern stepped aside and looked over at me to ask again, in a softly encouraging voice, "Sandra, would you like to feed your baby?" It took me a moment to understand that I was in charge. I pulled myself up even straighter and said, "Yes." And then, looking at the nurse, I said more strongly, "**I would like to feed my baby.**" Her cheeks colored and she spun around on the polished floor to retreat. I realized that medical staff were all aware of something I was not. *I had rights.* I had a right to information and to hold my child. The young doctor seemed entirely comfortable with this conflict and smiled at me approvingly. He was from California.

A short time later we could hear soft footsteps coming down the darkened hallway toward my room. This sound was accompanied by the sounds of a baby sucking on his fist and then howling in frustration and hunger because that tiny fist did not produce what he needed. *There was no alarm clock in sight.*

Many years passed before I considered how that young doctor who interned in Fort Smith, Arkansas, in October of 1967, had risked reprimand to give me hope and courage, and to offer Scott a full life. I don't know his name and have no way of thanking him for lighting that rebellious fire in my belly again. I have fantasized that we might somehow meet one day so that I could properly thank him and tell him about Scott's life.

The next day, they brought the papers for us to sign and I asked my husband what he was thinking. He looked at the floor for a moment and then at me before responding, "This is your decision to make." That is the moment I began to take charge of my world.

We took the baby home and were both quickly captivated by our beautiful child. His bruises healed, soft skull rounded, and the hole in his heart closed on its own. He smiled and then laughed out loud with a bubbling chuckle that seemed to start in his toes and move up through his entire body before erupting from his perfect little mouth. He wiggled and giggled with the joy of being loved.

There were still moments of fear and uncertainty after we took Scott home, but upon returning to California we had the support of family and friends, along with many dedicated professionals. As Scott thrived, my confidence grew.

We learned together, moving slowly but steadily through each stage of development. The toilet was our very best friend for four years, until we succeeded in 'potty training'. We practiced tying shoelaces every single day for two years until Scott could tie independently. Weeks later, I woke up to discover that somehow, during the night, he had forgotten how to tie. Scott curiously watched a tear roll down my cheek and then reached up to pat my arm in sympathy. A moment later, he held his foot up and gave our call to action, "Let's tie!" There would be no pity party. It took just a few days for him to retrieve that skill and he never forgot again. Of course, we now have the miracle of Velcro.

I haven't always been patient and am still haunted by times when I snapped at him or pushed him to "hurry!" when he was doing the best he could. Over the years there have been many mishaps, like getting kicked off a city bus and having to go to court; or being lost in a strange neighborhood; or making poor choices. Some are funny, others terrifying. Each has been worth the rich life Scott has enjoyed outside of an institution. I encouraged him to take risks and face challenges, and to experience both success and failure just like his beloved sisters, Kari, and Kristen, who truly adore him. Scott has taught us more about ourselves than we could have known without him.

At 49 years, Scott has a very important job cleaning restrooms and picking up trash at a highway rest stop. He gets up early and is ready to go every morning; completes his tasks with the help of a Job Coach and is proud to receive a paycheck. He can be funny, sometimes grumpy, loves to play checkers, work jigsaw puzzles, watch movies, bowl, dance, eat hamburgers, and look at pretty girls. Scott says he would like a wife and once had a lovely girlfriend named Melissa for several years. She dumped him when she realized he had a roaming eye. Scott seems to prefer women who look like Olivia Newton John in the movie *Grease,* which has significantly reduced the likelihood of a successful relationship.

Like other adult children, Scott moved out of his mother's house years ago. After unsuccessfully trying a group home, and then agency supervised supported living, he found stability and happiness in a private home with the support of a devoted caregiver and companion who lives with him. We have never once needed to remind him that it was time to eat.

After you became ill, some people expressed admiration for the way I have managed your disease. They said things like, "no one else" could have cared for you with such love, humor, or determination. I know this is not true but bask in their approval anyway.

What is true, is that I am rich with the experiences Scott and his friends provided. I had already seen and felt intact persons hidden beneath challenging brain conditions. Without exception, I witnessed them reach for recognition. I learned to stand up and speak for those without a voice. And I already knew that if I collapsed under the weight of sadness and loss, I would miss out on the laughter and those precious moments of felicity that appear without warning. These were the tools and the weapons they armed me with before FTD entered our lives. I knew I had no control over the outcome but would do everything I could to surround you with love and laughter along the way.

When we began our search for a diagnosis to explain your growing confusion, it was less frightening to think that it might be a tumor. We both knew it could be something else. As the technician prepared you for your first MRI, you gazed at me with still bright blue eyes. Struggling to find the words, you pointed your index finger at your head and said, "Maybe a lump, but not *that*. Not de... dementia." There it was again, *anything but that.*

I bent down to kiss your cheek and said, "We never know how high we can climb until a damn mountain blocks our path." You smiled, perhaps because I cursed. I prefer to think you felt reassured because, back then, you still knew Scott's story and how I had laced up my hiking boots in October of 1967. They still fit.

We Met in Church

CARE STAFF ARE getting to know you and your young age troubles them. We are all more accepting of dementia when it strikes the elderly. You are also an unusual challenge to them because of your size XL-Tall, and newly achieved heaviest weight of 185 pounds. They have difficulty redirecting you because your inability to comprehend language makes it impossible to explain things with words. Despite this, you often delight them by mischievously removing someone's sunglasses or hat to try on, or by walking off with a Dutch Brother's coffee that was left on a desk. When a chase ensues to retrieve the coffee, you still know how to duck and dodge to retain your ill-gotten bounty. If anyone wears a shirt or jacket with a hood, you can be counted on to gently pull it up over their head and then pat it firmly into place, with a chuckle. Gus-Gus is not appreciative when you pull his yellow doggy rain hood over his eyes.

Today one of the young caregivers is looking at photographs that I hung on your wall over a year ago. She gives me a sly glance and asks, "Are you a Cougar?" I laugh at her boldness. It's something I might have done.

"I don't think so. Cougars are hunters and I stopped hunting when I realized that the best things usually find me." Then I look directly into her eyes and reverently add, "We met in church." She giggles nervously and does not ask any more questions.

Religion is one of those topics that we should approach with caution unless, of course, one is mining for shared values in a new relationship. In this setting, full disclosure is critical to determining compatibility. We build the foundation for every relationship long before an introduction ever takes place. I remembered once telling you that I had some 'church trauma' I needed to disclose.

Looking at the photographs with her, I begin to think about

events that had propelled me into the building where I first laid eyes on you. When she leaves, I remove a picture from the wall and sit on the arm of your chair to share it with you. It shows us standing together on a cliff above the Pacific Ocean on our wedding day.

It was June of 2002. We had been a together for over six **years** and cohabitated for three. Selecting nice clothes from our closet, I wore a casual long skirt with a bright red sweater. You wore khaki pants with a dark, long-sleeve shirt that you dressed up with a broad smile and a wildly colorful fish necktie. We purchased inexpensive rings the night before at the Friday Night Art Walk. Neither of us was a fan of wedding rings and I wanted no *bling,* but you pulled me into a local shop where we found simple silver bands with an endless wave design etched around the surface. We agreed that this symbolized the ebb and flow of life, and of relationships. They were perfect for our little ceremony.

The next day, we casually stopped by our friend Don's birthday party to wish him well and then drove to our favorite beach close by. As we walked along a path to the cliff above, I picked a bridal bouquet of wildflowers which I later realized was slightly unlawful in a state park. After our ceremony, I tossed them over my shoulder into fingers of foam that reached up from the waves as they crashed against rocks below. There were just three close friends in attendance, Jay and Cindy to video and witness, and Tamar to perform the legal ceremony. We somehow convinced Tamar, who was raised in a conservative Jewish family (and served in the Israeli army), to become a Universal Life Minister so she could sign the necessary documents that would legitimize our marriage.

In this picture, the wind is blowing our hair and we are both laughing because part of your vows was a clever limerick. After the limerick, you stumbled through partial lyrics of a Sting song that you almost memorized and then looked into my eyes and promised, "Whatever happens, I know that I will always love you." As soon as Tamar declared us to be "a married couple" you signed with a flourish the document that gave me health insurance and declared, "Babe, you've got insurance!" The playfulness and lack of fuss on that day reflected our values. It was simple, loving, and honest. We didn't pretend to know what the future would bring, but we loved and respected each other and wanted to continue building a life together with both of us having access to health care. A few months later, we hosted a gathering to celebrate this wild leap of faith before surrendering to the demands of new jobs, my mid-life graduate program, and creating a home at the property we had purchased together.

Still sitting on the arm of your chair, I hold our picture up and playfully repeat, "We met in church." You used to roll your eyes in mock dismay whenever I said that to people. Today, there is no rolling of eyes as you watch me speak and then glance at the picture before turning your gaze back to the TV. It is showing a rerun of *The Golden Girls*. Your expression is flat, and the image of you and I laughing on a cliff above sparkling blue water is not enticing enough to hold your attention. We no longer share memories of that day, or of how we first met nine years before.

In November 1993, I was stationed at the entrance to Pilgrim Congregational Church so I could greet everyone and invite them to sign the guest book. We were all reeling from the tragic loss of our friend Ardeth's beautiful and free-spirited daughter, Jen, who sang like a songbird and had a brilliant smile that truly lit a room. She was a university student when she was hit by a car as she crossed the street one night after socializing at a local bar with friends. She died hours later from massive brain trauma. Both she and the driver had been drinking. In true Ardeth fashion, blame was not leveled solely at the young man who got behind the wheel of the car that killed her daughter. Instead, Ardeth focused on the high alcohol consumption of both young people and the resulting slow reflexes and poor judgement that led to the accident. A sad irony of Jen's death was that when she was a child, her father was also killed while crossing a street after leaving a bar late at night.

There were many familiar faces in the church that day, but I did not recognize yours when you arrived, late. You were the last person to come in before I gathered up the guest book and began pulling the heavy doors closed so the celebration of Jen's life could begin. I obtained your signature but didn't look down at it because I was watching you walk quietly around the back of the church and up along the far side of a sanctuary that was lined with floor to ceiling windows. The modest building was designed by Frank Lloyd Wright, a famed twentieth century architect who merged exterior landscapes with interior spaces. They built this one with no right angles, which I remember thinking was entirely appropriate for an organization that was attempting to guide people toward generosity and kindness. As you walked, soft sunlight filtered through the plants and trees on the other side of the thick glass to silhouette you. You were very tall and slender, and moved deliberately like an athlete. I later learned that you trained yourself to be slow and deliberate because of your tendency to trip on things. You were clean-shaven, except for a neatly trimmed mustache and carefully groomed soul patch beneath your lower lip. With an angular nose and sculpted features, you wore a dark suit contrasted by brown soft soled shoes that didn't match the suit. As you turned away from me, I saw a long dark ponytail trailing down the middle of your back. The sight of your ponytail caused another memory to take me back to an even earlier time in that very same room. This is how memories often find me.

Eighteen years before Jen's service, I crept into Pilgrim Congregational church as the last stop on a discouraging quest. I sat in the very back, next to those same windows, wanting to observe the congregation but be able to make a quiet exit if needed. Their welcome was warm but not overly solicitous. People were diverse in appearance, with some dressed in their 'Sunday best' while others were comfortable in jeans. They greeted each other, chatting until the organist began playing "Morning is Broken" by Cat Stevens. Everyone, including myself, stood up and started swaying and singing. Children remained with their families until the minister called them up to sit on the broad steps that led to the pulpit. He told them a bible story about kindness that, while tailored especially for young ears, was a reminder to us all. Looking around the room as children were bustling toward the hallway that led to Sunday school classrooms, I noticed a distinguished looking man several rows in front of me. He had a long ponytail trailing down his back, which was unusual in our rural community during that time. His hair was silver, not black, and I considered this long hair to be a positive sign.

Seven or eight years prior to that, my young family had been escorted out of a crowded church Christmas program we had been invited to. We were asked to leave because my college student brother-in-law hadn't had a recent haircut. He was clean and appropriately dressed but his hair covered the tops of his ears, which we learned was a disgrace. A grim-faced older man who was in charge of culling undesirables, notified him he was not welcome there until he had his haircut. When Jon obligingly stood to follow the man toward the door, we got up to join him. As we bumped and wove our way through the curious crowd, the absurdity of it hit me and I found myself taken by my own spirit. I began chatting a bit too loudly to my toddler son, whom I carried. Pointing to an image on the wall, I asked, "Do you think Jesus needs a haircut? You know he probably had beautiful brown skin, right? I wonder why they don't celebrate his birthday closer to the real time?" My first husband dropped his head and moved quickly forward while I hung back, walking slowly. I embarrassed him much more than his brother's shaggy hair.

I like to imagine that you would have smiled and walked beside me with your arm around my shoulders. It is also entirely possible that you would have later suggested my comments might not have been useful. You respected my need to confront prejudice and bigotry, but we sometimes disagreed about method. We had different styles. After telling this story to a friend, she insisted that the silver ponytail in Pilgrim church was an *invitation from God*. I am still envious of the pleasure she received from this certainty.

At your urging, I shared other church stories from my earlier life. Your eyes would widen with astonishment, or you would chuckle with amusement and encourage me to write them down.

At around age five, my very social eldest daughter began receiving invitations from neighborhood playmates to attend Sunday school. She begged and pleaded, becoming increasingly upset each time I said, "Maybe another time." I had spent years conducting my own search for God, who I hadn't found in church buildings. I did, however, discover compelling reasons for not letting her go without me. I still believed at that time that I had more influence than I ever actually did.

As I considered Kari's pleas, I reflected on my own experiences as a very young child when I attended church with my mother and grandmothers. I remembered it felt special. I learned to sit quietly and the music made me happy. I dressed up and wore shiny black shoes to stomp around in until someone scolded me. After church we often went to a little donut shop nearby where I would choose a chocolate-covered cake donut, creating a problem for whichever pretty dress I wore. My Great-grandmother, Anna Middleton, didn't seem to like me much but was always nice on Sundays. Even if I dozed during the sermon, I woke up for the singing. I knew all the hymns at an early age, which pleased her. My mother says great-grandma used to sing opera. I never asked where, but noticed she loved to dominate the voices around her in church. I would look up at her and try to extend my tones in the same warbled sounds she produced. She would smile at me, saying that I had "perfect pitch." The only other time I remember thinking she liked me was when I skipped out the front door shouting, "Get behind me, Satan! I'm Jesus's girl!" I already understood there was someone else I could blame for whatever mischief I had been up to. She repeated this story when I was older and asked me to move a soft bristled hairbrush across the terrible burn scars on her arms and upper chest.

I was told that great-grandma's clothes caught fire while she was cooking on a wood stove back in Colorado, when most of her nine children were still at home. People said she was a striking woman before the fire, and the nine children. At least one old photograph confirms this.

My Great-grandmother Anna Middleton, and Great-grandfather Thomas Middleton, who sometimes worked for the railroad, were desperately poor and lived on the west side of Denver. They often relied on gifts of used clothing and food from the local church. Great-grandma walked to church nearly every day. She played the organ, taught Sunday school, was a member of the Foreign Missionary Society and was also active in the Women's Christian Temperance Union, which I now find notable. The WCTU supported prohibition and the Nineteenth Amendment. Her activities frequently left the children, including my mother whom she raised, at home with the 'Black Irishman.' Thomas was my mother's grandfather but I never met him. I thought he was a Black man because of what they called him. It turned out that he had black hair and was rumored to have a black heart as well. My grandmother said that her father, "had the Irish thirst for alcohol." Thomas was also surprisingly handsome in an old photo, which appears to document eyes as cold as an icy window, and thin unsmiling lips. According to my mother, church gave Anna something that she desperately clung to throughout her life. Dana Carvey's "Church Lady" from *Saturday Night Live* might have been modeled after my Great-grandmother Anna, except that her absolute moral certainty was not an act. She was also massive rather than thin. I remember watching her eat astonishing amounts of creamed corn and mashed potatoes. She closed her eyes and smiled as she ate with the same transportive expression that took over her face when she played hymns on the piano. She was in her late 70's when she died of stomach cancer. I now wonder how different her life might have been if the only terrible scars she carried were from those burns.

I don't know how Thomas, the 'Black Irishman,' died. Nobody ever talked about him to me when I was a child. My mother says that she doesn't remember how he died, but I know she could never forget how he lived. After acquiring the emotional distance that eighty years provided her, she finally began sharing some of the dark and hideous secrets that had carved deep wounds and contributed to the hungry narcissistic hole in her psyche. These stories explained her desperate need for attention and approval, as well as her distrust, fear of abandonment, periodic depression, internalized shame, and unexpected outbursts of anger throughout her life. I have wondered if someone helped the Black Irishman with his exit.

I imagine that Anna's church was the eye in the hurricane of her life. Perhaps it was her only place of calm and safety. There were no laws to protect women or children and we take comfort where we find it. She has been dead for a very long time and I have only recently allowed myself to think about what it might have been like for her. Anna couldn't shield her children or grandchildren from undeniable harm, and she may even have surrendered them to it when she left for church meetings. But it was there that she might save herself and hope for sweet forgiveness, along with the promise of a new life for all of them one day. In Heaven.

After realizing that unsolicited invitations to Sunday school would continue, I decided my children should experience a church community of my choosing. It would provide a reference they could return to later, as adults, when they made their own decisions about religion and how it might fit into their lives. I hoped to find a church that valued women as equal partners, leaders, and decision makers; respected other cultures and faiths; honored and protected the natural world; and extended service, tolerance, and respect for difference into the broader community. I began visiting churches.

In one large palace of a church, a lively and exuberant young minister with an amplified microphone and PA system began pounding his fist and shouting at the eager congregation. He was worried that attendance had slowed and shouted that if their jobs kept them from coming to church and tithing on Sunday, they should "quit that job and God will find you another." There was rhythm and cadence to his performance. He had been practicing. Far too many attendees were nodding and murmuring in agreement and I could see that things might quickly becoming intolerable. I considered how I might slip out while challenged with maneuvering a diaper bag and nursing my hungry baby under the blanket that hid her and my breast. Realizing she would howl if interrupted, I decided to wait. As I settled back, I noticed a well-dressed grandfatherly man excusing himself over and over while pushing toward me past 15 or more people sitting in the very long pew. He stopped at my seat, towering over me. When I tried to swivel my legs to one side so that he could get by, he leaned down and asked in a loud whisper if I would "like to take my baby upstairs to the Mother's Room?" nodding toward a large window behind us that looked down on the sanctuary. I thanked him for being so thoughtful but reassured him we were just fine. He persisted, nervously glancing at my blanket, and telling me more firmly that he would show me the Mother's Room. I finally had a flash of understanding. It was not my comfort he was concerned with. A baby quietly suckling on a breast, even though not visible, was unacceptable in this House of God. I was stunned but gathered my composure and nodded toward another mother down the row who was also feeding her infant, but with a plastic bottle. I quietly suggested she might want help finding the Mother's Room. The man reddened and looked defeated as he straightened, shaking his head as he began his retreat. He pushed his way past the same people he had disturbed just minutes earlier. Of course, by then everyone nearby was looking at me and my blanket. I watched as he eventually rejoined two elderly women across the aisle. They were both glaring at me with pursed lips and grave disapproval. I saw that same expression on Great-grandma Middleton's face before she spanked me for wearing new pedal pusher pants that my mother had bought for me when I was four years old. "Good girls do not wear pants." Not only did those women not come to my defense, but they also appeared to be directing the man who had approached me. I understood that they believed they were keeping me and themselves safe. Bad things can happen to women and girls who do not conform. By then I knew that even worse things can happen to those who do.

I locked eyes with them and sat in quiet défiance, waiting for the church Gestapo to arrive and remove me and my offending breasts from their midst. I had lived in San Francisco during the mid- 1960s and was prepared to go limp in passive resistance. When security people failed to appear, I felt compelled to stay with my now sleeping baby and endure the rest of the dangerous little man's sermon. To retreat after taking such a stand would have been unacceptable. I still have difficulty deciding which cross to hang myself on.

Another notable church experience occurred when sweet and innocent Kari was *saved,* along with a dozen or so other children bused in from a housing project across town. They were marched proudly from their Sunday school class and joyously paraded in front of the whole congregation while everyone smiled, clapped hands, and praised Jesus. The children grinned and skipped, delighted with the attention. When I later retrieved Kari and her older brother, Scott, from their class, she was very excited about celebratory ice cream (which I knew was strawberry because it had dripped down the front of her dress) and about being saved. When I asked her what she was saved from, she thoughtfully raised huge blue eyes to the sky before confidently answering, "From God." Scott and Down syndrome had not been marched in front of the congregation but had also clearly enjoyed celebratory ice cream. Perhaps they realized that he, at least, was already saved.

I tried a Unitarian church that seemed casual and inclusive. However, when I was invited to participate in a discussion about the nature of suffering, I was told very publicly that I was *cynical* for wanting to explore the statement that "*all* pain and suffering is self-imposed by our beliefs and expectations." The small audience was mostly white and middle-class, like myself, with basic needs met. I had hoped to discuss this complex issue on a more practical level. While I agreed that our beliefs and expectations shape our experiences, the reverse is also true. I suggested that traumatized children and adults might not be able to grasp this concept until they have healed. The discomfort in that room was as palpable as it had been when I was ten years old and instructed to leave a Presbyterian Sunday school class after asking how we could know *for sure* that God is real? I sincerely hoped that someone there would have an answer for me. It was humiliating, and this was not how I wanted my own children's questions to be responded to. I fervently hoped they would have the courage to ask questions.

Of course, when I mentioned being kicked out of Sunday school, you exploded with laughter, saying, "Nobody ever asked questions like that in my Sunday school classes." You were so entertained by my church stories that I also told you about being suspended from a high school Social Studies class for refusing to withdraw *Existence of God* as my chosen example for a speaking assignment. You pointed out to me that a recurring theme was emerging.

We were asked to select a topic that was commonly thought to be true but with no evidence to support it. I had planned to point out that some things can be true even though evidence hasn't yet confirmed it but was interrupted before having the opportunity. I was very nervous. The teacher, who I later learned was a devout Christian, was as red-faced as I was when he demanded that I come up with a different example. I seriously couldn't think of one because my brain froze. Pointing at the door, he told me to "leave this classroom and do not come back." They suspended me from school for only a half-day because it was a public high school and the principal intervened.

My parents drove the 60-mile round trip to meet with the principal before taking me home with them. Mother sat in angry silence during the ride but I could tell that my dad was trying not to smile. When he finally spoke, he said, "You need to learn when to keep your mouth shut." I reminded him that it was a *speaking assignment.* He surrendered to laughter while shaking his head, which made me laugh too. It helped me feel less embarrassed and confused.

When I told you this story, you kissed my forehead saying, "I'm sure glad they couldn't shut you up, like a good little girl." Not everyone agrees. These missed opportunities to explore thoughts and ideas caused healthy curiosity to transform into open rebellion.

You and your buddy, Matt, were altar boys and enjoyed lighting candles (fire), and the pretty girls (more fire). Attending just one church throughout your childhood, the only embarrassment you recalled was that your family always walked in late (a trait you later claimed to have inherited). You could think of only one other interesting church story, when your mother insisted that you meet with the minister after she learned that you were having sex with your high school girlfriend. You told me that the minister privately suggested you would be "trapped by that girl" and encouraged you to end it because you were "college-bound and had a bright future." You didn't remember him expressing concern about your girlfriend's future and I don't remember asking if you ever shared the minister's comments with her.

Just a year or two out of high school, while still in college, you returned to church for the white wedding your first wife dreamed of. You adored her parents and wanted to please them as much as her. That first marriage didn't last for all the reasons young marriages often end. You admitted to being self-absorbed and immature, and that you each betrayed the other's friendship and trust. We agreed it might be wrong to think of these marriages as failures. Life is a cycle of beginnings and endings, and the pain of that relationships demise was a catalyst for growth. You declared yourself to be a "better man" after that and she went on to create a new family for herself.

You returned to church again when your lovely second wife, whom you connected with at a class reunion, also wanted a church wedding. When you shared this, I felt a flare of judgement. I knew that by then you were skilled at birth control and had also denounced religion. Declaring with a sheepish smile, that you were "bewitched by her beauty" and agreed to a church wedding because you wanted her to be happy. I thought this was as good a reason as any.

I was there to witness your face break into a wide grin when your third partner announced she wanted to stand on top of a cliff above crashing waves with a congregation of flowers and grasses swaying in the wind while a forest of redwood trees witnessed from the surrounding hills. She was not pregnant and needed nothing from you but love, respect, and health insurance, which was also a very good reason for marriage. Especially after purchasing property together. There was no church in sight, but that little ceremony strengthened a deepening commitment and inspired the continuation of a loving adventure that is now ending in a way that was not on any list of possibilities.

After discovering Pilgrim Congregational Church, I was better able to appreciate the value of an extended community. This was, in part, because of a beautiful, grandmotherly woman named Rosemary, who gently pulled crying and writhing, 10-month-old Kristen, out of my arms when I came to retrieve her from the nursery because she refused to settle down after several Sundays. Rosemary urged me to go back to the sanctuary and "enjoy the talk." When I hesitated, she said encouragingly that my baby "will learn that other people also love her and can keep her safe." For three more Sundays, Rosemary would take a wailing Kristen outside to the garden and walk with her along the wooded paths throughout an entire sermon that failed to drown out her shrieks. Rather than disapproving scowls, people smiled and reassured me. Rosemary never lost patience and Kristen eventually surrendered to her love. After that, I could relax while she played in the nursery. I also watched the older children taking nature walks outside those beautiful windows.

I learned that the silver-haired ponytail belonged to a man named Alan. He and his wife, Molly, were both architects who had different faiths and alternated Sundays between each other's churches. Alan and Molly became my good friends outside of church. You also knew them briefly and was present when I asked Alan about the ponytail which he had long since cut off. He told us he had been working as an architect in a rural area during construction of a community college that took several years to complete. The construction crew had a habit of making offensive comments about men with long hair, using derogatory terms like *hippy, dirt,* or *queer.* Alan stopped cutting his hair. The longer it got, the quieter the workers became until the comments stopped. I wanted people like Molly and Alan in my life.

I found a safe and nurturing place at Pilgrim Congregational Church during the period that my first marriage was disintegrating. Like my grandmothers, I found refuge. I also found that I could sit through a service that had some relevance to my life. Yet, try as I might, I never felt the presence of a biblical God others seemed to commune with. The people were intelligent and kind, and they served each other and their community in important ways. After other churches rejected them, Pilgrim welcomed a group of gay community members to worship with us, and to also use one of our meeting rooms. I first learned about Jewish traditions when a Rabbi came to share the story of Hanukkah with us. Guest speakers were welcomed and we also learned about Buddhism. They encouraged us to notice similarities and respect differences. I like to imagine that Pilgrim Congregational has continued inviting representatives from other religious groups to balance the rhetoric and neutralize the division and fear that is being encouraged.

After several years, I felt it was dishonest for me to continue. I was sitting in my favorite pew at the back of the church and gazing out those same old beautiful windows, when the saying "there are many paths to God" drifted into my mind. I needed to move on. Life was my path, and I would discover many sacred places.

Leaving Pilgrim Congregational behind as a fond memory, I invited mystery to sit on my shoulder again and whisper into my ear. I don't need to own it or give it a name, but I honor the life force that courses through each of us to shape our lives, our universe, and beyond.

My Christian friends tell me that God will welcome me back whenever I am ready. I appreciate the additional layer of insurance.

Aside from welcoming the entertainment these stories provided, you were understanding of my quest. As a scientist, you understood the need to question. A good scientist spends his life searching for new information that might disprove his own theory. Religion tends to avoid that.

We contemplated together that in another 7.5 billion years (give or take), scientists expect our sun and earth to die their own natural deaths, just like everything else. I've since read that the atmosphere supporting human life is not expected to last more than just 1 billion years, and this is only likely if we begin now to live more responsibly and reverse the accelerated heating of our climate, and poisoning of our own air, water, and food supply. I now understand that it is also possible for the earth to be knocked off its axis or lose its magnetic field. We could be hit by another huge asteroid, or rogue planet, or experience catastrophic volcanic eruptions, again. Of course, there is also the increasing possibility that we will save nature the trouble by blowing everything up with our clever nuclear arsenal. *Could anything be more absurd?*

We humans are hard-wired to group and rely on each other for both physical and emotional survival. We need communities like churches, but whatever origin story we adopt, it only makes sense to live life with reverence. I personally believe that Eternal life will be achieved when we die and again become a part of that larger something in a universe we don't yet understand. We are extraordinary beings created from the earth, rather than the earth being created for us. I could be wrong.

Digging into thoughts and exploring ideas about religion was important to our friendship, Randy. Sharing the same core values created increased intimacy and trust. We were each guilty of irreverence about many things, but we shared a deep respect for the wonders of life. When I revisit these conversations in my mind, I feel like we are getting to know each other all over again.

After Jen's service, I asked Ardeth who you were. She reminded me they had talked about you, Randy Brown, many times. I remembered then that you and her partner Dave worked together on small hydrology power projects requiring permits on streams throughout Northern California. Dave described you as a "smart and witty guy." He did not mention how nice you were to look at. I later learned from Ardeth that at the time of Jen's death you were struggling with an unhappy marriage. During that same period, I was nearing the end of a long and loving, but increasingly unhealthy relationship.

Ardeth's grief over losing Jen became less raw with time. When her humor crept back, she teasingly accused me of "lusting over you at her dead daughter's funeral." I don't remember feeling lust as much as intrigue. I should have paid closer attention to noticing that you were late. We were first introduced over refreshments after Jen's celebration of life but you had no memory of that meeting when we were introduced again, a year or so later.

The second time we met, both our circumstances had changed. You had separated from your wife and filed for divorce. I had ended my relationship and moved back into my own home. I invited Ardeth and Dave over for dessert on Thanksgiving Day and they brought you along as a stray. We sat outside because it was unseasonably warm, and I have a picture of you sitting on the railing of the front porch on my 1930s three-story cottage. You unleashed your ponytail and appeared unwieldy with your hair flying about. You were mostly silent that night and surprised me when you spoke up, mentioning that you'd been to my house before. I'd forgotten that months earlier, you had picked up an extra bed while I was at work. Ardeth suggested I donate it to you instead of Goodwill because you had left your wife and the boys nearly all the furniture. Since you were sleeping on an inflatable camping pad, I was happy to leave the bed, along with some extra linens and towels, on the porch while I was at work. I couldn't have known that one day you would smile cagily at me while patting that same mattress and say provocatively, "Your old bed wants you back."

We got to know each other over the following year. Ardeth

would invite me for lunch, or dinner, or an evening of music. At the last minute, she would say something like, "Randy is in town and wants to join. I hope you don't mind." Dave was doing the same to you. It was eventually revealed that after our 'First Thanksgiving' as we later called it, you made a comment to them that you found me "interesting and attractive." With that, Ardeth put on her matchmaker hat and Dave became her accomplice.

Having known each of us for years, they realized we could be great friends, if not more. They had not considered it because of our twelve-year age difference. Without their tampering, we may not have discovered our similar values and interests. Both of us enjoyed music, dancing, concerts, and theater. Each strongly political, we had spirited debates. We craved being outdoors and started going on hikes and bike rides together. I taught you to ski and then you learned to snowboard. I will never forget your giant body falling, over and over, on the Bunny Hill at Mt. Shasta. They moved you to a separate area so fear of being crushed did not distract the little kids. I loved that you weren't afraid to look silly and you certainly did.

We were both playful and lusty. We discovered that we had each made mistakes we weren't proud of and it was in sharing those stories that we grew even closer. I admitted to you that I'd gone through an angry period of 'Roaring and Whoring', treating men like they so often treated women. I had numerous lovers before settling into a pattern of serial monogamy. Without a hint of judgement, you responded with a smile, "Practice makes perfect!" Nothing either of us had said or done was shocking enough to offend or frighten the other. This was remarkable. Also remarkable, we never used something we'd shared in confidence as a weapon during a disagreement. Trust took root. We challenged each other yet enjoyed our differences. We first became friends and then became lovers. It felt safe.

The first time we made love was on your 38th birthday. I

had recently turned 50. It was passionate, playful, and altogether glorious.

I made a dinner of grilled wild salmon with pan roasted red potatoes and asparagus. I baked a mixed berry pie (your favorite) for dessert, jabbing a single candle in the middle of the latticed top crust. Singing a silly 'Happy Birthday' to you as I lit it, I said "Make a wish!" You leaned back with hands laced behind your head and looked at me with a thoughtful expression. "I'm wishing for happier times." After you blew out the candle and took a bite, you smiled and added, "I think my wish is already coming true." Because it was a warm summer evening we ate outside on the porch and never stopped talking. We talked about politics, work, the coming water wars, music, and kids. After dinner we washed dishes together then went for a walk. We shared a tiny glass of brandy before you prepared to leave. We were standing at my arched gate when you leaned down to kiss me goodnight and whispered, "Thank you for a wonderful birthday." This kiss was different because I didn't pull away. It lingered, becoming slower and deeper. You never made it to your truck that night and didn't go home for two days.

You were fresh out of an 8-year marriage and a couple of short rebound relationships. Joking about these, you said, "I scared them off because I was starving for affection." I had finally unknotted the emotional strings that kept me tied to my previous relationship. Together we tumbled through a window of opportunity that had opened for us. We would not have had the space to discover each other if we had not each been courageous enough to create it.

How Can I Help?

I AM OUT of town and my neighbor, Kathy, just texted to say she would bring in a package that UPS left on my porch. It is a small kindness for which I am grateful. My new neighbors are helpful that way.

I have had a lot of help in my life. First, relatively decent genetics gave me a healthy body and brain. Second, despite her own challenges, my mother loved and cared for me. There were great public schools and early childhood education that enriched me and kept me safe while she worked. The only 'fast food' I remember eating was an occasional hot dog from Casper's on Shattuck Avenue, near our apartment in Oakland, California. The skin of a Casper's hot dog popped when you bit into it and the juice ran down your chin, even if you were very careful. I've never since tasted a hot dog so delicious.

I don't remember Mom reading for her own pleasure, yet she read stories to my brother and me, and on Saturday mornings took us to the Public Library for story-hour. A love of reading developed and has nourished me throughout my life. Our mother joined the YMCA where I learned to dance the Waltz Clog in shiny black tap shoes. They also taught me how not to drown in the pool, which has worked so far. I remember being glad that boys were in a separate class because they swam naked. When I asked why, the answer was "Boys don't need to be covered up like girls." Of course, I have many more questions as an adult. There was little or no cost for these classes because we were poor. I remember Mom telling a lady at the YMCA that she was a "war-widow" which brought comforting pats. Considering what we know now about PTSD, it may not have been entirely false. What she did know was that being divorced did not reliably generate sympathy.

I didn't miss a father until I was older and saw other little girls with theirs. As a single woman with little money, Mom needed to work. However, her low wages were still enough to pay for housing, food, and transportation, and she had access to childcare and healthcare, which was a tremendous asset for us all. My brother and I attended a Lanham Child Care Center while she worked. These were the first universal childcare programs in the United States. Established during WWII, they were created and funded by taxpayer dollars so women could step into the jobs men vacated when they were drafted to fight. I have wonderful memories of being there. My mother was able to support us and we were excited to go there every day. Our education began in pre-school and continued with after-school care when we were older. There was reading, math, games, art, music, and safety. My brother and I went to public schools and colleges and grew up to become taxpaying adults who stayed out of prison, which points to money well spent.

In adulthood, my parents loaned me the $300 down payment to purchase an FHA mortgaged house during my first marriage. The equity from that house made it possible to build a larger and nicer house a few years later, which produced even more equity. This was how we began to build assets.

I have had help with multiple moves, which is a measure of true friendship. I had help fixing stuff. Stuff was given to me. I've had help with childcare, and faithful friends who helped me through tough times. I once received emergency food stamps after my purse was stolen out of my car during a period when I was living paycheck-to-paycheck. When the State of California insisted that I become a Real Estate Broker or work under a broker's supervision, I wore out several nice brokers until my brother allowed me to operate my Property Management business under his broker's license. This relieved me of the trouble and expense of acquiring one myself. (I did not intend to develop a career in Real Estate.) He even declined taking a percentage. His generosity probably kept me in that business much longer than I might otherwise have remained. It provided consistent income and flexible hours while raising children on my own. *These are not small things.*

You have forgotten this history and I don't want to. I want to be reminded that nobody ever gets anywhere, not ahead or behind, completely on their own.

After a couple of years together, our romance and friendship were thriving. My Property Management business was not and I needed to make some decisions. While you were settling into a new job and community on the coast, I was suffering from classic 'burn-out' even before unexpected personal challenges took me into the danger zone. Each event tested my values, my resilience, and our relationship. When the dust settled, I was surprised to find you still standing beside me. Instead of running the other way, you would appear on the porch and encourage me to talk. If I didn't want to talk, you would stretch your hand out and say, "Let's go for a walk."

During our second year, I had a laser resurfacing of the skin on my face. The doctor gave me a discount because it was his first time using that tool. You later said that "he should have paid you for the practice run." The laser burned too deep, causing hideous swelling and copious oozing, accompanied by a week of excruciating pain. I was an unrecognizable, disgusting, mess. Friends came and went during the week, bringing food and helping to change dressings while avoiding eye contact and shaking their heads as they left. You came on the weekend and sat with me and my huge, seeping, Jack-o-Lantern face. We read, listened to music, and watched movies. We talked about everything *except* what I had done to myself.

When my skin healed, it was smooth and unblemished, but seemed to have stretched from the excessive swelling. They forgot to tell me that I was to sleep upright for the first week. I convinced the doctor to tighten it up with a 'tuck' at no extra charge. He wasn't happy, but he numbed the skin behind my ears and flipped me upside down in a special chair before pulling a piece of skin from each side and unceremoniously hacking it off. He then stitched it together behind each ear. It took all of thirty minutes. I thought my skin looked great while ignoring the knot behind my ears. You made no comment. For months.

One day we returned from a bike ride and were sitting outside across from each other at lunch when you leaned forward and studied my face for a long time. I thought that I must look pretty good when you ended your scrutiny by musing, "I wonder why you thought *that* was a good idea?" You had that now familiar half smile on your face and your eyebrows arched in a mockingly curious pose. There was no venom in your tone and I melted into wild giggles. No one else could have lightened the feelings of shallowness and utter idiocy I had been consumed with. I had precancerous spots removed every year and convinced myself that doing them all at once made more sense than removing a few each year for the rest of my life.

I am happy to report that the skin on my face has remained cancer free. However, I must also acknowledge that the *real* reason I burned it off was that I liked the idea of having new younger skin for my new younger lover. It was pure vanity.

It took much longer for me to confront my insecurities about our age difference. I announced to anyone we met that you were *younger,* just to get it out of the way. Even after we were married, I would repeatedly remind you that 70 was going to look way older than 50. I was preparing myself for the possibility that you might leave the crone that I would surely become. Now you have, but not on purpose.

It turned out that you never thought much about those spots and wrinkles. You said that you noticed "What I thought about, my laugh, facial expressions, my spunk and intelligence, my strong legs, and my cute butt. Years later, when the freckles and spots returned, you would kiss my cheek or forehead and say, "I can't decide which is my favorite flavor." Spots were not exclusive to my face. One night we were lying in front of the fire watching a movie when you pulled up the back of my shirt and began gently tracing an invisible line, up and around, back and forth, across my skin, pretending to connect the dots. It turned out to be a surprisingly erotic thing to do. For a long time after that, if someone referred to 'connecting the dots' you'd say, "I've done that!" and give me a wink. I began to trust that you accepted the whole package of me, including my many, many, imperfections.

Also, during that second year, I had emergency surgery for a large fibroid tumor that was causing heavy bleeding and serious anemia. The hospital insisted that I put thousands of dollars in co-pay charges on my credit card and I began making payments. An unexpected drop in income resulted in quick depletion of my savings and in just a few months I was at risk of losing my house and my business. A friend who had experience in such matters, encouraged me to file what later turned out to be an unnecessary bankruptcy. It was one of the most demoralizing experiences I have ever been through. The judge took a personal interest in my case. Suspecting me of "hiding assets," he showed up at my home, unannounced and without a warrant, to peer through my windows. Through it all, you would comfort and reassure me I was doing what I needed to do. You would say, "This is why we have Bankruptcy Laws," or "The mafia was indicted for charging interest rates like that credit card company."

Soon after the bankruptcy, business magically increased and I paid back much of the discharged debt. I remember you studying my face and asking, again, why I "thought that was a good idea?" This time you asked in a genuinely curious way. I replied, "Because I can." I had felt ashamed, but you said you *admired* me and leaned over to stroke my cheek with a tenderness I hadn't experienced. It felt deeply sincere and there was no price tag attached. When I feel unsure of my motives, I sometimes call up that moment.

The third year we were together, I made a stunningly stupid decision by moving forward with a real estate trade before having a signed contract. Based on a verbal agreement and promise to sign "soon," I uprooted Scott and his roommate and moved them into the main part of the 'new' house. I moved myself into a small apartment upstairs so I could be close, but not too close. I was already spending extended periods out of town and this allowed me to come and go while keeping watch for safety issues without interfering in their routines. I meant for the house to eventually be shared with other roommates who also qualified for supportive caregivers, rather than a typical agency-run group home. When I became their landlord, there would be no worry about future rent raises or property sales that could result in loss of housing.

The refusal to sign came after appraisals were lower than expected. When the stability I was trying to create for Scott was put in jeopardy, I immediately reversed the moves based on violation of our verbal agreement and forced her to vacate my smaller house so that Scott and his household goods could be moved there with his support staff still in place. I moved my own household possessions into storage. *You and other friends helped with the equivalent of four moves in less than six months.* Few things are less romantic than moving. Four moves might easily send most friends into hiding. It was the end of a friendship, but not ours.

That was the start of a wonderfully stable period for Scott. During the turmoil, he lost his roommate, but we found a new caregiver who moved in with him and I became his landlord as originally planned. I house-sat for my close friend, Marcia, who had accepted a job out of the area, took care of her cat and prepared her house for sale, which allowed me to begin thinking about the changes I wanted to make in my own life. She gave me the time and space to consider my options more carefully.

Despite this positive outcome, I felt tremendous guilt over twice upending Scott and his roommate, which had been difficult for each of them. The friendship betrayal also took a toll and after listening to me vent about that, you pointed out that I seemed mostly angry with myself. I scoffed.

One day, we were sitting on a large rock after hiking up a hill to look across the valley at the magical sight of 14,000-foot Mt. Shasta. Wrapped in a brilliant cloak of snow, it glowed pink where the late afternoon sun was hitting the ridges while shadows deepened the crevices. It was getting cold and you pulled me in close with your arm around my waist as we sat in silent reverence for where we were at that moment. After a while, you looked down at me and casually said, "I was always curious about your friendship with that person." It was out of context but I knew who you were referring to. You pointed out that we "seemed to have very different values." I shrugged, "She made me laugh." You said something about "expensive entertainment" and then encouraged me to forgive myself for having a lapse in judgement. It was when you raised your voice in frustration that I realized how much it was also affecting you. "You didn't betray anyone or make promises you didn't keep. You didn't stiff a contractor for thousands of dollars or forget about remodels without permits and then slander an appraiser who just did his job. Nor did you fabricate ludicrous stories to shape opinions in the community." You got my full attention when you pointed out that everyone else had moved on, while I was "stuck." I realized you were right. I *was* mostly angry with myself. After a long pause, you quietly asked, "Do you think you can get past this?"

I nodded yes and admitted that I was glad she had not signed the agreement. I also wanted to be forgiving and offered "She believes she did her best." You gave a low chuckle and said, "Some people just pretend to do their best. They should be avoided." There we were sitting up on that rock, laughing again. I wasn't pretending when I assured you that I was over it, and you were visibly relieved.

I continue to be amazed at how you never lost your footing with me. Or your sense of humor. My trust in you grew and my love continued to deepen.

As Scott and his caregiver settled in together, I still struggled to go to work every day. I'd rather starve than go to a Chamber of Commerce meeting and I was doing little to promote my business. I had always promised myself that when my children launched, I would go back to school. My youngest daughter, Kristen, had just graduated from college and moved to Colorado for a job. Kari was married and living out of state with her military husband. Scott was now settled, and I began to consider that maybe it wasn't too late.

Rather than push the thought away, as I had done for years, I started to seriously consider the complexities of dissolving a small business and returning to school to restart my education and embark on a new career at 50+ years of age. After one of my musings, you leaned forward to touch my shoulder and asked, *"Sandi, how can I help?"*

I knew that you weren't trying to save me. You just wanted me to have what I wanted. Other friends thought I was crazy to think of going back to school at my age. They were afraid for me, thinking it was too late to start a new career. They wanted me to put energy into building the business which seemed secure to them. *You thought it didn't matter what they thought.* You believed in education and supported my desire to do something that made no clear sense to anyone but myself. Even if it meant the end of our relationship. When you reminded me that "life is short" I felt as if you were holding a very heavy door open just in case I decided to walk through it.

At age 53, I completed college application forms. If I was accepted into the university closest to you, we agreed that I would live with you and we would see how that worked for us. If I was accepted into Chico State, it would bring our relationship to an end. I was accepted into the school near to you, and you grinned while pointing a finger at your head to point out that it had advantages Chico did not.

Over the next few months, I prepared to leave the community I had been a part of for more than three decades. When doubt crept in, I would repeatedly remind myself that life is a series of adventures, and success is not measured in dollars.

Light from a Burning Bridge

I AM BOUNCING around to music while cleaning our very neglected house. Stopping from time to time to edit, I begin to copy select songs from an old playlist on your computer to a new one that we can play on speakers in your room at memory care. We have discovered that music still has some relevance. Songs somehow connect you to otherwise unavailable language. While you cannot retrieve or comprehend words and names in conversation, you frequently bring up and sing partial lyrics of familiar songs with no prompting. The only way I can now get you to say my name is to sing, "It's Sandi, Sandi Girl" to the Howdy Doody tune, which you happily mimic. My efforts to inspire you to sing these words are another blatant manipulation that I justify because you respond with such a big grin. We are both happy with this little ditty.

I have shuffled through a fraction of the 3,000+ songs you saved on your computer when Elton John's voice floods the room. He is singing "American Triangle" and I must sit down.

The last time I heard this song was two years ago when we were still living in our home together. By then, your language was severely limited and you expressed few emotions other than frustration or giddiness. I walked into your study to find you leaning back in your chair with your hands hanging helplessly at your sides. You wept while listening to Elton's song.

I realized that you remembered what had happened and connected this song to that event. Your hands reached up to hold onto my arms when I wrapped them around you from behind. I laid my head on yours and asked if you were "thinking of Gary and Winfield," You nodded '*yes.*'

Elton wrote and recorded "American Triangle" to commemorate the death of a young college student, Mathew Shepard, who was abducted, robbed, and murdered for being gay. Newspaper articles described hours of torture, saying he suffered massive brain injuries and was tied to a fence overnight in freezing temperatures on a windy plain in Wyoming. His brain died there while the rest of his body waited for the hospital. This happened in October of 1998. The ignorant brutality of it shocked and galvanized much of the country.

We followed the story closely at the time. Mathew's murder ignited social justice and equal rights advocates. With the help of his family and friends, the media contrasted his joyful and loving nature with the violent acts and hateful attitudes of the young individuals who had enticed, tortured, and broken open his skull. We asked each other, "Who taught them to think this way?"

This event pushed the debate over civil rights for LGBTQ citizens and there was political movement to add sexual orientation and gender identity to the list of federal protections. Some states did so after communities rose on behalf of LGBTQ brothers and sisters who were being discriminated against and denied full rights of citizenship and recognition of value as members of humanity. Tragedies like this can jolt people out of complacency and inspire change. It can also encourage more violence.

Less than one year later, on July 1, 1999, our friends Gary Matson and Winfield Mowder were found murdered in their rural home near Redding, California. They were also targeted because they were gay.

The phone call came while I was still in Redding cleaning up business affairs and saying goodbye to associates and friends. I had raised my children there and was leaving behind many friends and memories as I launched myself into academic life at the university, and a new domestic partnership with you. I was feeling melancholic when I arrived at the office early that morning. It was before business hours but I picked up the phone when it rang. The voice of my office assistant and good friend, Diane, was almost a whisper as she said, "Roger found Gary and Winfield dead this morning." She pushed each word out like it was sticky and refusing to leave her tongue.

Diane was in shock as she tried to explain how Gary Matson's brother had driven to their home after being unable to reach them by phone and hearing a strange voice recorded on their answering machine, saying they were out of town. Gary's brother, Roger, found them in their loft bed covered in blood. We would learn that the murderers had forced them to climb into their bed, which was 7 feet off the floor, while they stood on chairs and shot them, over and over.

I was numb with confusion and disbelief. We had all been together just a week or two before and I could not imagine anyone in our community being capable of doing such a thing.

I had forgotten that the people who murdered Mathew Sheppard looked like people we pass every day on the street; shop with at the grocery store; and pray with at church. They seemed to be regular people who decided they had the right to assault and kill someone who was different from themselves.

I immediately called Gary's ex-partner, Marcia, in Davis where she was living and working. Marcia and Gary had remained close. She had just heard the news from Gary's father, Oscar, and was wailing hysterically. I asked her if I should come and she begged, "Yes! Please, please!" I closed my office and recruited our mutual friend, Heidi, to drive the 150 miles in record time, somehow avoiding a speeding ticket. We spent the next 24 hours taking turns sitting on the floor, holding Marcia. When we could no longer hold her, we just sat with her and bore witness to her grief. Her pain was too immensely personal for us to join. We also grieved, but I had never seen anyone surrender to such raw emotion. Marcia wailed and moaned "Why?" and "No!" howling like Janice Joplin. She dove deep into her own lake of despair and then surfaced to crawl and claw at the floor. She would do this for an hour or more until she wore herself out, then slowly grew quiet, curling into a fetal ball to rest until another tsunami of emotion welled up and pulled her onto her knees again. It was like she grieved for all of humankind, that such mindless hatred could so viciously take someone precious to her, and to their daughter. Around 4 AM, Marcia suddenly realized Clea did not yet know that two of her three parents were murdered.

Clea was in Mexico, immersing herself in the language and culture by living with a Mexican family for an extended period. News of the murders was just appearing in media across the U.S. and Marcia became frantically focused on reaching Clea before she saw it on television or in a newspaper. She got a call through to the host family, telling them what happened. She asked them to keep Clea away from the TV and newspapers, then booked the next flight. When Heidi and I drove her to the airport, she could barely walk upright. It had been over 24 hours since she slept or ate and she could hardly choke down water. I explained the situation to the flight attendant and another passenger, who kindly promised to keep an eye on her.

Marcia was the first to tell Clea. She brought her back home to what remained of her family amid a homicide investigation and media storm. The public would not know the horrific details of what had occurred until the trial. Those of us in the inner circle knew, and this knowledge would burn into our minds and shake our faith in humanity.

The murderers were identified as brothers, Benjamin Mathew Williams, and Tyler Williams, who were both tracked down and convicted. Multiple news reports described them as polite, clean-cut, and enamored of Neo Nazi and White Supremacist movements. Christian Identity ideology, a belief system that most Christians reject, also influenced them. They might now be described as "radicalized Domestic Terrorists" although this still seems to be mostly reserved for violent people of other faiths. Domestic terrorists of this variety are now considered to be one of the largest growing threats to our democratic republic. They do not believe in Democracy.

News reports, articles, and court transcripts describe how the Williams brothers were convinced of their own moral superiority and resulting violence through select scripture and radical literature. In addition to killing Gary and Winfield, they were convicted of firebombing three synagogues and burning a women's clinic that performed legal abortions. Authorities found a hit list of Jewish leaders that they also planned to kill. They believed their actions were God's judgement but seemed unwilling to give their God much credit for his omnipotent ability to sort things out himself.

A *Salon* article titled "Poster boys for the summer of hate" (by Sam Stanton - Gary Delsohn), was published in October of 1999. It describes these events and provides a small window into the Williams brother's lives. Wikipedia.org offers a more extensive breakdown. As children, they were mostly homeschooled and socialized primarily with people from their church. Their mother was a public-school teacher with access to other young minds. A recorded jail conversation revealed her telling Benjamin (Mathew) that she heard he "took out two homos." Their father was reported to be more upset by their sloppiness in getting caught, than by their violent crimes. Benjamin was known to have homosexual tendencies, which would surely have tormented him.

In the end, there are no rational answers. While interviews and news stories pointed to the likely genesis of their hatred and resulting violence, one absolute fact was held under the glaring light of the trial: *Two precious human beings had been murdered. Their lives taken in a horrific and ultimately senseless manner.*

Benjamin Mathew committed suicide in jail while awaiting trial. He had attempted to escape, seriously injuring a guard with a homemade hatchet. The younger brother, Tyler William, will likely be in his 80's before he is eligible for parole. Their parents were said to have quickly moved out of the area. In the end, a daughter lost her parents, parents lost their sons, a guard was permanently injured, friends, family and an entire community suffered betrayal and devastating loss because of these acts.

When the song ended, I asked if you remembered Marcia, pointing to her picture on the bulletin board above the desk. You nodded, repeating "Marcia."

Marcia and Gary were passionate, creative, and unconventional people with uncompromising ethics. You were cautious when I introduced you. Caution transitioned to a warm camaraderie during our first evening together. Respect and affection grew with each gathering that followed. Admiration took hold when you learned their story.

They met in college at UC Santa Cruz when they were just 18 years old and became friends and lovers. It was many years before Gary could admit to himself, and then to Marcia, that he was gay. He had tried very hard not to be. By the time he told her, they had created a life and a daughter together, and Clea was still very young. Gary was traveling back and forth between Redding and UC Davis to pursue a master's degree in Environmental Horticulture, when he revealed to Marcia that he had met and fallen in love with Winfield. She went into a spiral of despair, feeling betrayed and terrified of losing her family. She admitted being jealous of Winfield and heartbroken for Gary, her partner and best friend, who had spent years suppressing his true self by trying to be someone he was not. While an outspoken advocate for social justice, Gary had forced himself to hide in that proverbial closet so as not to hurt Marcia and other people he loved. Of course, they suffered anyway, perhaps even more because of the secret.

Marcia's love for Gary and Clea tamed her anger and grief.

She was able to forgive him by realizing that if Gary had been allowed to be true to himself, he would not have been untrue to her. She was able to also forgive herself for missing clues that had always been there. It would prove to be more difficult to forgive the ideology and culture that nurtured the violence that would one day take his life.

Marcia invited Gary to bring Winfield home to meet her and Clea. She desperately wanted to preserve her family and decided that if she could just expand herself enough to accept this new member, they could all raise Clea together. After Gary graduated, they tried sharing a household for a brief period, until Marcia realized just how emotionally brutal it was to live with Gary and his new partner. My friend Rox is fond of saying, "Sometimes, when you take the high road, you get a nosebleed." Marcia purchased a place of her own so Clea could go back and forth between her two homes. Gary and Marcia resumed their friendship and took co-parenting to the next level.

Winfield turned out to be kind, witty, and entirely lovable. He quickly grew to adore Clea and they all refocused on her needs. Marcia healed, while friends and family accepted and appreciated Winfield. He had been a hair stylist and began to take care of Clea's beautiful white-blond hair. He served as fashion consultant, baked birthday cakes, and made Halloween costumes. Winfield was also gregarious and charmed everyone who met him. Clea grew up with three parents and an extended family who were all devoted to her. They nourished her mind and allowed her to experience a family that actually *lived* values of unconditional love, respect for difference, and service to community.

You and I shared many meals and gallons of wine from the Matson Winery while enjoying intelligent and always spirited conversations around their dinner table. We were with them on Thanksgiving Day when a strong earthquake sent everyone diving under the table during one of those conversations. You and Marcia became close, sharing political affiliations and passion for science. After a few glasses of wine, she would lean toward me and whisper, "Let me know if you tire of him."

The community credited Marcia and Gary with establishing the Carter House Natural Science Museum, where Marcia served as Director. Carter House was later absorbed by the current Turtle Bay complex, which was a difficult transition for Marcia when she was forced to watch her beloved grass-roots project become something very different. Gary was also the passion and vision behind establishing an Arboretum nearby, as well as the local Grower's Market which he and Winfield participated in until their deaths. The Grower's Market is where they met the brothers who murdered them. With Gary's encouragement, Winfield, who struggled with dyslexia, worked very hard to receive a bachelor's degree in Anthropology. The last time I saw Gary and Winfield was when we gathered at Oscar's home for a dual celebration of Winfield's birthday and graduation from college. I baked a birthday cake and decorated it with piles of chocolate "mud" frosting and tiny bones and digging tools. It was great fun and we were all proud of his accomplishments. We could not imagine that they would soon be gone.

The lengthy investigation and trials added years of additional stress, which delayed healing for Marcia. She and Clea wanted the death penalty taken off the table. They didn't believe that it was rational to kill someone for killing someone.

Less than four years later, Marcia would also be dead. She did not smoke and exercised daily. During that time, she developed pulmonary fibrosis and rheumatoid arthritis flared to attack her joints with a fierceness that curled her hands and feet. Marcia had cried every day for three years and many of us believe that a failed immune system due to unrelenting stress and grief caused her death. Just as she was beginning to pull out of her persistent state of despair, she became physically ill. In a matter of months, inhalers no longer worked for what she and her doctor thought were asthma attacks. She soon required oxygen 24/7 and began the application process for a lung transplant. Clea was home visiting her mother when she started gasping for air and made the decision to call for an ambulance. I was told that the last words Marcia whispered in the ambulance were, "*Clea, Clea.*" I am not alone in my belief that Marcia should be counted as an additional victim of hatred and bigotry. If you include Tyler Williams who remains in prison, five lives were ended as a direct result of hate-fueled ideology.

Clea was left without parents to share and guide her through transitions into adult life. She has grown into a lovely and successful woman with a clear mind of her own. While sharing many of the same values, Clea has somehow tempered any inclination toward the wildly passionate ways of her beloved parents. Like you, she has a different style. I hope she will one day write about the remarkable family that loved and shaped her.

Reflecting on all of this, I remember that we also lost our friend Heidi, who had shared the frantic drive to Davis with me. Heidi was only 53 when she died. She was the director of an environmental camp for grade schoolers and had become friendly with you when your stepson Christian was attending the camp and you volunteered to teach the kids about fish-cycles and stream habitat. You were still married to Jordan's mother during that time and I didn't know this history when I met you. I later remembered Heidi joking about the "sexy biologist" whom she wished wasn't married. I laughed and quipped, "Yup. The good men are either gay or committed." Sometimes they are in transition.

At some point I had mentioned to Heidi that I was spending time with a nice guy from out of town, without saying your name. One evening, you and I walked into a restaurant together while she was there with other friends. We greeted her in unison, calling "Heidi" and then looked at each other and laughed because we didn't realize that we both knew her. Rather than smiling and waving, she appeared upset and rushed out of the restaurant.

We were dumbfounded. I asked how you knew her and it was then that I realized you were the man she had talked about. She wouldn't return my calls but I knew that her reaction had nothing to do with you, or me. Heidi desperately wanted a family and used to ask me why she was unable to establish romantic relationships with men who attracted her. She was smart, beautiful, and accomplished. I had no answers.

Heidi eventually created her own family and we were thrilled when she got back in touch with us after adopting her first baby. We welcomed her with open arms, and she brought her young daughter to visit us on the coast. We had a lovely time and hoped things were back on track for resuming a friendship. However, our busy lives had moved us further apart than we realized. We saw her infrequently and the last time we were together, she had adopted a second baby from Nigeria. She was thrilled with her little family and not prepared for a relapse of breast cancer. Heidi died unexpectedly of pneumonia while recovering from chemotherapy. I have heard that her little girls are now being raised by friends in a rural community with few Black faces but am confident that her love still surrounds them and will help them find their way. Our grief over losing Gary and Winfield, and then Marcia, resurfaced with the news of Heidi.

During those hazy days after the murders, it was you who reached into the suffocating cloud of grief that enveloped me. Once again, you took my hand and walked me outside so that I could feel the earth, see the sky, and breathe the air at the beach or the forest. You had not yet forgotten what I needed.

Now, all these years later, I attempt to reach through a cloud of dementia to give you what you need. I believe that the tears you cried while listening to Elton John were not exclusively for Gary and Winfield. They were also for Marcia and for Heidi, but ultimately, they were for *yourself.*

It was during that same early stage of disease, while you retained some comprehension of what was being taken from you, that you spent frantic hours on the computer searching for, but never locating, your old college friend, Barrett. By then you had lost your job, driving privileges, and many of the words that would have allowed you to express your anguish. This was also when you began gathering up pictures of yourself along with anything that had your name on it, and taping them to doors, walls, windows, and lampshades. You were trying not to disappear.

A few weeks after I found you weeping with Elton John, we were sitting together on the bench above our little frog pond when you slid your arm around my shoulders and pulled me close. I melted against you, soaking up the rare affection. I was hungry for that. You felt fully present when you said, "I'm sorry." I asked, "For what?" and you answered, "My brain." You pointed your index finger at your head again, but this time you had your thumb up and middle finger bent like the trigger of a gun. I pulled your hand down and wrapped it with both of my own, bringing it close to my heart. I replied, "I love you. I can't imagine *not* being here for you."

This would be the last time you shed tears or expressed concern for anyone's feelings, including your own. I had no way of knowing how much I would come to rely on my own tears to lubricate and soothe the chaffing and frustration that would accompany the sadness and growing challenge of making sure you are safe and cared for.

As I think back to that time, I realize that any remaining hesitation over leaving Redding completely vanished after Gary and Winfield's murders. My attachment to that community dissolved with their deaths and my way forward was illuminated by the bright light from that proverbial *Burning Bridge*. I had no idea how things would play out but understood that life would keep taking shape if I just had the courage to step into it.

Oh, What The Hell

Go for it

Frog Whispering

EVER NOTICE HOW 'Oh, what the hell' is usually the right answer? My friends Eric and Martha presented me with this question engraved on a slate stone, which I display in my kitchen. They know I have found tremendous satisfaction in taking certain uncalculated risks, even when things have turned out differently than hoped. Sometimes we overthink things.

I disregarded my internal warnings when I entered that nearly disastrous house swap. But when I followed the intuition to reverse it, everything fell into place for all of us, including my former friend.

Ignoring all advice, I dissolved my business and moved into your 'Little Blue Box' on the Northern California coast to begin a new life with you. It is a decision I never regretted.

At an age when many people are preparing for retirement, I enrolled in a university. Taking my time, I repeated classes in subjects I had enjoyed and took extra classes I wanted to explore. In the spring of 2002, I graduated with a bachelor's degree in social work and then went on to complete a master's program through California State University, Sacramento. It was an achievement that you encouraged me to believe I deserved.

And then, when Scott and his caregiver moved into a new house without stairs, we sold our separate properties and combined resources to buy the Big Pink Box in the Wetland, which led to our decision to legally wed. These were all tremendous risks that we both met with a cavalier, "Oh what the hell!" It felt right. If we needed to make a change in the future, we agreed to decide together how best to move forward.

The house was not exactly pink but more of a puking mauve color. It was much larger than we needed and a huge project, but a solid deal. Or so we thought. It was also in a great location, close to our work. Best of all, it was next to a forest and a wetland that was protected and could not be filled like the land they built the house on. It was private yet close to everything and loaded with potential.

We celebrated your 44ᵗʰ birthday by placing our signatures on documents to finalize the sale. This was done despite a visible mess and promised repairs that were not completed. We forgot that there is nothing like the possibility of losing a sale at the last minute, to inspire people to do what they agreed to. Instead of refusing to sign the papers, we accepted new promises and chose to trust. It was the only real mistake we made during our dive into a more committed life together.

We jumped in and started swimming, almost literally, when an unexpected downpour caused the basement and garage to flood. The French doors also leaked, spreading water several feet into the living room and onto a carpeted area which, after pulling it up, exposed that this was not the first saturation. Someone had improperly installed the French doors. We tackled one thing at a time, according to urgency, and gradually made it our home.

During the first showing, I remember standing on a deck overlooking the 1/2 acre back yard and pointing to a large wet spot in the soil at the base of a hill. This section was full of tree stumps, non-native blackberries, and wild mustard. I excitedly declared, "It wants to be a pond!" You seemed not to hear me as the agent effectively drew your attention away. I was persistent, repeating myself while tugging on your sleeve like a child. "It WANTS to be a POND." Your distracted response was "Yeah, maybe..."

One of the first things we did, after hauling out a huge dumpster of trash, was to rent a bobcat and dig a hole at the base of that hill. Our friends, Jay and Cindy, took turns with you on the bobcat. As you dug, water seeped into the hole. Within a day or two the pond was completely full. It turned out that there was a spring just above that spot and the soil itself was mostly green clay. It held water like a potter's dream. We never lined it and it never went dry. For overflow during storms our friend, Paula, suggested digging a winding little stream to direct water back down to the adjacent wetland. You did that and then built a sweet little foot bridge that was practical and picturesque.

Our little pond became an obsession, and the hub of what would become mostly native garden beds surrounding it. This was one way to mitigate some of the damage that had happened by building the house there in the first place. It was also a creative outlet. I moved some native plants, including grasses, reeds, cat tails, sword ferns, spiraea, equisetum, and Douglas iris up from the forest and adjoining wetland to reintroduce vegetation around the pond. But you would not let me put anything other than a few large rocks into the pond water. You kept saying that it would "take care of itself." You wandered down to check it every evening, coming back to report on what that small body of water had enticed. Sometimes you'd call me down to point out a little water beetle, then sliders and other aquatic insects. Then dragon flies, salamanders, newts, and snakes; then California red-legged frogs and Pacific tree-frogs (also known as Chorus frogs) appeared. Eventually we had a couple of turtles, mating mallards, various hawks, and owls, and one Great Blue Heron who frequently stopped by for a frog snack. Numerous other birds came to drink and merrily bathe in our little pond. A wide variety of furry animals also meandered through the garden and to the pond for a drink or a bath. Until the frogs became our constant companions, I had no idea how many things ate them. I kept reminding myself of what ecologists have learned: Predators and prey are equally necessary parts of the same organism. They keep populations healthy and in check.

We dubbed you *The Frog Whisperer* because you became skilled at mimicking just the right tone to excite them. You would sneak outside at dusk, stand very still, and then call, *"Erreet, Erreet,"* until one frog could no longer resist the challenge and croaked a response. This led the entire pond into a deafening chorus. The frogs were so loud during mating season that we had to disclose them in our rental contract with tenants of the guest apartment on the lower level of the house. Our friend, Anne, presented you with an official *Frog Whisperer* cap that you wore with pride.

Bear wandered through, and we would note the different personalities. Some were bungling and destructive, knocking over bird baths and statues, while others would gently sniff and touch, but not destroy. There was a doe we named *Mary Without Joseph*. Mary showed up pregnant each winter for several years in a row, producing twins. We watched as her yearlings hung around until she ran them off. It was time. We had more than one mountain lion. However, the garden was mostly enjoyed by birds of all kinds, and foxes, skunks, raccoons, possums, mice, rats, chipmunks, squirrels, and feral cats that were sometimes trapped and taken to the animal shelter. House cats belong in houses.

Two different students from the university studied our pond and found it to be especially prolific in native vegetation, pollinators, and wildlife when compared to other small ponds in our area. One said this was likely because we controlled dogs and cats and didn't use chemicals for lawns. You were very proud.

We planted a row of rhododendrons that escorted visitors down the long driveway to the house. There were native azaleas that smelled heavenly in the spring, vine maples, alders, dogwood, hazelnut, ceanothus, and elderberry. We planted flowering currents, huckleberries, oak leaf hydrangea, nine bark, penstemon, monkey flower, aster, lupin, poppies, California fuchsia, and more grasses and ferns. We also created sections of raised beds for blueberries and vegetables, which we had to protect when our conversations with the deer were ineffective. During an epic battle with gophers, you would blast music from the movie *Caddy Shack* and channel actor Bill Murray, but without the explosives. Finally surrendering to the gophers, we let them have what they wanted. We would sit up on the deck and watch certain plants wave and wiggle, getting shorter and shorter, until they were pulled completely down into the tunnels like a Bugs Bunny cartoon. Those varieties were not replanted and we lived in relative harmony. I placed wire barriers in the soil under the things they couldn't have, like blueberries, carrots, potatoes, and other vegetables.

By the time we left it, we had painted the Big Pink Box a neutral tan and the decks and rails were repaired and stained. We moved soil away from the house and drainage issues were resolved. We replaced roofing and gutters, flooring and leaking French doors. Princess wallpaper was scraped off or covered, new appliances installed, and walls opened. Outside, we built retaining walls and paths. The beds were filling in. There was more to be done, but it had become the gathering place you dreamed of. It was also the place where our relationship flourished.

Gus and I both became ridiculously excited the first time we heard Pacific chorus frogs in a pond near your assisted living facility in Southern Oregon. We were living in the parking lot and the frogs sang me back to memories of happy times with you at our house in the wetland. The last memory of our little pond was when our friend, Eric, waded out to the middle to retrieve the adorable metal duck that another friend, Pam, had created by welding garden tools together. Eric rescued it from the large rock island where I had placed it. This duck now lives under a pink flowering Nine Bark in my lovely cottage garden. It doesn't appear to be unhappy.

Four years after your diagnosis, I listed our home for sale and it sold before a sign went up. The universe was nudging me again. Over the next month, our phenomenal friends kept showing up to help me sort through the remaining pieces of our life together and move them to Southern Oregon so I could be close to you while you received the care I couldn't provide. I said goodbye to our house, gardens, and the frogs who didn't respond. I didn't have your special tone.

Lucky Man

I HAD TO wrestle myself out of bed late this morning so won't be coming to visit you until afternoon. Rain and wind pounded on my window all night and I slept very little. I half dreamed, half imagined raindrops were tiny fists hitting the glass, knocking and knocking, demanding to be let in. I tossed about in my warm bed, agitated as I always am during such storms. I thought about the people I used to know who may still live outdoors, trying to stay warm and dry in such weather. I wished you were here to stroke my back like you used to and begin to remember how we once looked this demon in the eye. Words from Walt Kelley's often-quoted comic strip, *Pogo,* pop into my mind: "We have met the enemy and he is us."

As I settle into my coffee cup, sipping and brooding, my eyes focus on water that is puddling on the patio. This is the kind of rain that finds your skin through layers of clothing and fills shoes that squish when you walk. Persistent saturating rain causes fungus to grow in uncommon places if one cannot get dry quickly enough or stay dry long enough.

I allow my mind to drift back just a few years to that beautiful sunny day in San Francisco when we meandered down the Embarcadero together, dodging strollers, skateboarders, joggers, and panhandlers. Your disease had progressed to what I estimate was mid-stage. The need for physical care was minimal, but you were child-like in your fascination with everything and it was difficult to keep you off the boat ramps. We needed to cross the street, but you no longer understood the rules of doing so safely. You were unafraid of most things, including traffic. When the stick person on the green signal began walking, I said, "Let's go!" grabbing your hand and swinging it in a playful manner as we joined other crossers. You enjoyed this and we were soon on the other side of that very wide, extremely busy, street. We began walking in a quieter area near our hotel when you stopped and pointed into an alley toward a recessed doorway where a man sat tucked in against the door. He had a filthy sleeping bag wrapped around his shoulders despite the warm day. His hair was matted and he did not make eye contact.

You asked, "What is that?" Your tone and expression were flat, but you knew something wasn't right and no longer had the words to express it. I tried to move you along but you resisted, repeating "What is that?" Your hands gestured toward your own clean clothing and then to his. You looked at me like I should do something.

I grabbed your hand and tugged, "We shouldn't bother him," which you didn't comprehend. The man was not panhandling, yet you pulled your wallet from your pocket and took out the $20 bill I always made sure you had there. You said, "There is this" and walked toward him. It felt intrusive and a little dangerous, but I couldn't hold you back. The man saw the $20 and very slowly stood up. After a long pause, he cautiously reached for the money. Once grasped, he turned away and began to drag his bag down the alley while responding to voices only he could hear. You attempted to follow him until I pointed to a sandwich shop behind us and pulled you in that direction.

We were soon munching on beautiful sandwiches made of soft chewy rolls stuffed with roasted vegetables and melted cheese. As I watched you happily engage in your favorite activity, there was no doubt in my mind that you still remembered...

I started my new job at the center a decade before FTD entered our lives. We were both working long hours in new positions and workdays often ended when one of us called the other on the phone. You usually gave in first and I would sometimes have a spoon of peanut butter in my mouth when I answered your call. I would mumble, "Are you hungry yet?" You would laugh,

"Are you eating peanut butter again? Meet me at the pub in ten minutes."

We would sit at the bar and eat an assortment of appetizers for dinner while exchanging highlights of our day. There was something about being away from home that allowed us to focus more closely on each other. The one who had the best story didn't pay. It was a *law*, just like the law mandating that whoever cooked did not wash dishes, although we often did both together. You pretended my stories were the best even when they weren't. Your income was considerably higher and you would wave your wallet in mock surrender, "Okay. Okay. You win again. Put that one in your memoir!" It was a joke.

Despite having seemingly opposing missions, each of us believed our work was important. You worked to protect habitat and strengthen natural systems that were critical to the survival of animals that were being threatened by unchecked human activity. You were taught to focus on the health of the whole system rather than individuals. In a natural system, weaker individuals often die or are eaten before they reproduce, which strengthens the system. You once, very cautiously, suggested that shoring up weak individuals from an invasive species (us), that is over-populating, over-consuming, and destroying habitat, threatens the entire system (earth) that everything depends on.

Contrarily, I worked to strengthen the frayed safety net that is critical to marginalized individuals from this most destructive species. Unlike natural systems, social systems artificially control the distribution of resources while the identification of 'weaker' individuals is influenced by culture, prejudice, and greed. Eugenics exposed the dangers in attempting to override nature to fulfill narrow social and economic desires. There are plenty of examples of how we might heal our environment and control our population, while also recognizing the value and contributions of individuals outside the mainstream. People at the bar would sometimes join our discussion.

We found common ground when agreeing that if we repaired our social systems, we might also repair the natural systems that are being decimated to create monetary wealth. Sometimes we would end our discussion with sheepish smiles and toast Michael Moore, "How much is enough?" We knew we couldn't solve these problems by ourselves. It was time to get the car keys.

I remember thinking on the way home that you always became more interested in individuals after I told tales of the intelligence, creativity, and resilience I witnessed at the center. Sometimes you would try to guess who I was talking about but I would never confirm. Even when you guessed right.

My first day was nearly my last. I arrived an hour early, before doors opened to volunteers. An alcohol and urine saturated body lay in front of the door, waiting to greet me. It turned out to be a common occurrence and there would sometimes be more than one. This one was swathed in a cocoon of filthy blankets and the stench was overpowering. No hair, skin, or other body part was visible, and there was no movement when I stepped over it. I detected soft breathing so decided to talk to someone before calling 911. My sensitivity to the smell of unwashed bodies was the first thing I believed I would be unable to adjust to. It turned out that much of what I believed about myself, and about this population, was wrong.

When staff began arriving, I asked about the body that had magically moved away from the doorway. The answer was the same, "Oh, he sleeps there." I already knew that sleeping overnight was a violation of the lease. It was not licensed as a night shelter. I also knew that if you make exceptions for some but not others, resentment builds. A slippery slope.

When doors opened at 9 AM, I jumped for cover as a dear volunteer with strong lungs and a joyful heart took her place at the front desk and began greeting every single person who entered by shouting, "**Welcome home, sister! Welcome home, brother!**" Over and over, and over. I appreciated the cheerful sentiment but to my knowledge, nobody except paid staff had a key to the front door. It turned out I was wrong about that too. In any case, I am not good at promoting other people's fantasies. Only my own. I started a list of topics for the first staff meeting.

Shouting dependably inspires more shouting and the center became a cacophony of noise as people, dogs, washing machines, meal preparation, and other activities each contributed their own unique pitch. When a community member's frustration appeared to be escalating, one staff member began to shout, "May Day! May Day!" While successfully alerting other staff to potential violence, he also risked inciting the same, along with heightened anxiety throughout the building. There were occasional dog fights and people fights. Some cut ahead of others in line, running for the shower and locking the door before the next person could make it. Others would find a safe corner and wait until the few aggressive folks had their needs met before venturing to the desk to sign up for services. Some never left their corner, preferring to sit quietly, hoping for invisibility. Drug use and psychosis often shared the same space, and it was sometimes difficult to discern which was in charge at any given moment.

By the time doors opened each morning, we had fed breakfast to a crew of volunteers who were signed up for daily tasks that kept the center running. Rather than wandering the streets, these folks were able to stay all day in exchange for their contributions. They also received extra food, job skills and work references. Kitchen workers were assigned to prepare, set up, serve, and then clean up after feeding more than 100 people the only hot meal many would receive each day. Showers and bathrooms required continuous attention. Normal laundry operations were overwhelmed after a heavy rain, when sleeping bags, blankets, coats, and socks, would be hanging throughout the building.

Cleaning, sweeping, mopping, and general maintenance inside and outside was never-ending.

Every morning there was a line of people and their belongings winding up the walkway. Some were housed, most were not. They lived in cars, garages, or on someone's couch, while others camped under freeway overpasses, in the forest, or near the beach. They came alone, coupled, in small families, or grouped as travelers and families of choice. There was a mix of races and genders, but the majority in that rural area were white males. We had a few elderly people and some young people, always too young to be on the streets. Young women often arrived with children of their own. Many had run away or were pushed out by their families. Others had no family. A surprising number were aged-out of the foster care system without any supports in place to transition them into adulthood. This has changed since that time, but I am still haunted by the memory of a difficult young man who had been with the same foster family since infancy. When the payments stopped on his 18th birthday, they handed him two paper bags containing clothing and other personal items before dropping him off downtown. By the time we met him, he had been on the street for over a year, and alternately victimized or protected by other street people. He was inattentive, impulsive, developmentally delayed, and socially inappropriate. His facial features were uneven and he could barely read or make change. We were able to have him evaluated through the Regional Center where he was diagnosed with Fetal Alcohol syndrome (a permanent developmental disability) and assigned a Service Coordinator who arranged for housing and services. Others were not as fortunate.

Initially, people came in for the toilets, showers, laundry, and food. Sometimes they just wanted to get out of the cold. Case managers would sit at lunch and engage them in conversation, scattering little seeds of opportunity. We invited them to join a program that would teach basic skills like budgeting, filling out applications, job experience, or housing readiness. We helped retrieve birth certificates, lost social security numbers, and identification cards. We provided bus passes for medical appointments, social services, and job interviews. Mental health outreach arrived in special vans to offer treatment but were spread thin and unable to come often enough. Sometimes they were ready for rehab. Still others wanted help getting back to families in another city or state, and we were able to negotiate *one more chance* for them. Most people had no family to negotiate with. A maximum-security prison in another community would regularly bus newly released prisoners to our door during the night. We had no idea what their offenses had been but could be certain they were serious.

The longer folks remained on the streets, the more their mental health deteriorated. Some became angry and demanding, while others surrendered all hope. Like birds with clipped wings, they waited for seed to be scattered. What they believed about themselves had manifested.

I ended my first week by firing a long-term staff member after discovering that everyone did not feel safe in that place of refuge. Stress, anger, emotional, spiritual, and physical anguish dragged through the door along with meager belongings. It swirled through the air and was sucked into our chests every single day and we needed to minimize rather than increase its momentum. We all needed to feel safe there.

I had to terminate this beloved staff after she assaulted and injured one of the young 'travelers' who had reached for something without asking. After uncovering a string of past incident reports, I discovered this was not the first time she had established her authority by physically notifying people who didn't acknowledge her status. She was also kind and revered in the homeless community, sometimes taking new people under her wing. But she was loyal to her own and made sure they received special treatment and supplies. There was a political hierarchy even there. After I let her go, local followers rose in protest and there were threats. We gathered staff and volunteers to process their anger. I never wavered in my decision, repeating that *"everyone* needs to feel safe." Their distrust of me was palpable, yet we managed to get through it with a full crew of volunteers available the next morning. That evening, I discovered a deep scratch that ran the entire length of my car. When I got home, you strongly encouraged me to reconsider the zero benefits of that job. I agreed to think about it.

My first all-staff meeting brought clarity and confirmed what I already suspected. *I was entirely unprepared.* Everyone was worried about change, yet few understood the center would close if things stayed the same. They ran it like a clubhouse which encouraged member participation and a sense of ownership, but without a full understanding of privacy laws, funding, and contractual requirements. Members were also very attached to the outgoing director, who was passionate and personally invested. They hadn't voted for this new person (me), who felt it more helpful to clarify that the center was not a home, but a community-funded opportunity where they could rest in a safe place, or work for long-term change that might lead to acquiring a real home, with a door they could lock.

They hired me for the position of Executive Director because no other rational person would do it for the wage offered. A friend had convinced me I could save this "desperately needed" program. She checked off my qualifications: I cared about people. I had management, accounting, and supervisory experience. I had worked with low-income families in HUD housing and had a long internship with Child Welfare. I was familiar with social services and resources. And, I had just applied to a graduate program in Social Work. It would be valuable experience. I agreed to do what I could for a year or so. I was there for three and it was the hardest job I have ever had.

Along with brutal hours in a stressful environment, the Director was charged with mitigating a growing swell of controversy and opposition that had been building in the downtown community since the program was established. Despite my qualifications, I also had serious shortcomings. I was not a public speaker who could garner support by giving inspirational talks. I was not a good networker and tended to ignore influential individuals, because they were "important." Worse, I had zero patience with business owners who shouted into the phone about "dirt bags." Thankfully there were many in the community, including business owners, who supported the program and treated everyone with a measure of respect. We began to work collaboratively to solve problems and I promised to do my very best. You agreed to be supportive if I didn't put myself in danger.

My third week at the center, I stepped over the original body again, whose name I learned was Alex. There were also two new bodies who had slid in on that slippery slope of implicit permission. I said, "Good Morning," and received just two greetings in response. Alex remained silent, as usual. I scheduled a meeting with case management staff for the next day and started with a question: "Why are we allowing people to drink themselves to death on our doorstep?" They knew I was referring to Alex and the answers were still uniform. "He can't participate and has nowhere else to go." I asked a second question: "What have we done to encourage him?" They insisted again that he is "incapable of participating." My final question was: "How do you know he can't participate?" No one responded.

Staff agreed to collaborate and come up with a list of resources we might offer anyone we found sleeping on site. A few days later, Alex was once again alone on our doorstep and staff prepared for an intervention. They cared deeply about him and there were tears and doubt, even anger, as they reluctantly followed me outside to circle him with support. Each had something to offer.

Unlike the others, I had not actually met Alex, who was a 'mystery bundle.' I called his name several times before he finally stirred and gently asked if he would talk with us. A moment later the blanket moved aside and he sat up, brushing very long, very matted, black hair out of a movie-star-handsome face. I looked into the most startlingly vivid green eyes I have ever encountered. His gaze seemed clear and steady, like it was coming from somewhere far beyond the chaos of his current condition. I explained to Alex that we could lose our lease if he kept sleeping there and asked if he would allow us to help him. Our lead case manager assisted him to his feet. He had clean clothes ready and helped him into the shower. Over coffee and breakfast, he gathered as much information as possible about Alex's past, his family, and his medical history. It turned out that Alex was a Veteran who had seen and done things that no one should ever have to. He suffered from PTSD and at some point, also began hearing voices, which he discovered could be quieted with alcohol. I would meet other people like Alex, who treated their mental illness with alcohol or other substances. We arranged for a psychiatric work-up and he received an additional diagnosis. After medical detox, he enrolled in a residential rehabilitation program but left early and returned to the center. He brought new medications with him and they were impressively effective. Over the next year, Alex allowed himself to be guided back to the land of the living. He made halting but steady progress, taking two steps forward and one step back. The dance of recovery. We danced with him the entire way, never giving up. Alex eventually acquired housing, a driver's license, and a job working nights as a janitor. He later explained that this job didn't last very long because his medications required periodic adjusting and, "you know... the schizophrenia makes people uncomfortable." The way he externalized it struck me. The disease was not who he was, nor did it belong to him. I never heard him say, "*my* schizophrenia," or "*I am* a schizophrenic."

My last contact with Alex was several years after I left the center. It was after midnight when our home phone rang. I don't know how he got that unlisted number but the voice was unmistakable. I knew he had left the area but he updated me, saying he moved to be close to his father. He had been thinking back to his time at the center. It was 2 AM, but he wanted to say, "Thank you." He thanked me for "saving his life" and I reminded him that the whole team had pulled him to his feet. He was the one who decided life was worth living. Quiet for a moment, he finally said, "Well then, thank you for making me laugh again." We laughed together one last time and talked a bit more. It seemed that he was under the influence of something... perhaps alcohol or his medications. I didn't ask. It sounded like he was still doing the hard work of managing the illness that would remain a part of his life. I continue to be touched by his gentle spirit, sense of personal responsibility and gratitude. A true hero in our midst.

When I hung up the phone and came back into the bedroom, you sleepily propped yourself onto one elbow to watch me walk around the bed. I slid in behind you and snuggled up against your back before telling you why the phone had rung so late. You pulled my hands in around your chest and said, with more than a hint of sarcasm, "I know other people love you too. I just wish they wouldn't call in the middle of the night to tell you."

I did one thing that was related to public relations by resurrecting a newspaper column that the previous director had begun years before. We used this, along with an occasional newsletter, to provide statistics and personal stories that the community could relate to. I described how the funding was being used to help people find nourishment, treatment, jobs, and housing.

Often, you would weigh in on which stories to select for the article. I told stories of desperation, but also of humor, kindness, and generosity. There were people who gave up their only sleeping bag on a freezing night to someone who was ill or injured. Over and over, I watched people with almost nothing, share what they had with someone who had less. They reminded me of *Grapes of Wrath* and how John Steinbeck told us who we could count on for help if we needed it. Poor people understand how *one small thing* can mean survival for just one more night.

I told very human stories, like the one about a woman who slept on the concrete floor of the center every morning because she walked all night, every night. After being sexually assaulted more than once, she was too terrified to sit or lie down in the dark. Some, mostly young women, would attach themselves to any man who offered safety, trading sex and sometimes affection, for protection.

I knew a sweet middle-aged man, a veteran, who was afraid to come inside the center because he might get trapped there. He would stand at the window after lunch until someone noticed him and prepared a food box for him.

There was a very elderly man who was housed nearby and struggled to the center every morning, bent over, and leaning on his cane. He would hobble to the bread rack that was stocked each day and select a loaf or two to carry home. He never spoke.

A housed mom brought her kids in because she wanted them to know that we are all part of the same human family. Others came at the end of each month when they ran low on food. Many had jobs. Several families lived in cars and would come to shower or share a meal. One man, who was preparing for a job interview, was allowed inside before we officially opened so he could shower and select new clothing from our donation closet. After he cleaned up, his little girl who was around four years old, proudly beamed up at him with big brown eyes and asked, "Daddy, do you feel 'hoomin' again?" He got the job and we all felt more human.

I met several people who were on spiritual quests. One had walked for over a year, starting on the east coast, picking up trash along the way and eating only what was offered, not unlike the

Buddha. Another always carried a bible under her arm and held it up as a shield whenever she felt threatened. It seemed to work. Yet another worked his way across the country, found us, and never left. He was a poet at heart and became one of our most beloved and valued employees.

There was a middle-aged woman who ran from her home to escape a violent relationship. She had no idea what to do or where to go but was taken in and protected by a group of young travelers who brought her to the center. We were able to help her into a shelter with safety protocol and case managers to assist.

I became close to a lovely and intelligent young woman who cheerfully survived on the currency of her body, which her father and brothers had taught her to do at a young age. She was comfortably housed but volunteered at the center every Friday to shave and cut hair for anyone who wanted it. Some showed up just to watch and be in her presence. She once worked as a hair stylist and had briefly been homeless after leaving a violent "older man" who she had married right out of high school. She declared that marriage be a "dishonorable contract" saying, "Nobody owns me now." She also had a serious addiction. One day, I asked when she would be taking back that part of herself as well? A few days later, I heard that she had gone into rehab. My good wishes went with her.

There was the time I arrived late for a community meeting after traffic had backed up because a brand-new sky-blue Mercedes Benz had stalled in the middle of the road. Its well-dressed owner was frantically trying to push it while other drivers, including myself, were trying to get around him. Suddenly, a beat-up old van sputtered to a stop, and a scraggly group of vagabond travelers poured out like clowns in a circus. Smiling and waving, some efficiently directed traffic while others surrounded the car to push it out of the way. There are villains and champions everywhere. Sometimes they are mistaken for each other.

Not all stories were appropriate for the newspaper. One day

I was home catching up on paperwork and having a much-needed quiet day when my phone rang. This should only have happened in an EMERGENCY. It became clear over time that many people have a different concept of what that might look like, particularly when one's entire life is an emergency. One of our mature woman volunteers was on the line. She was known to be a bit rigid and was clearly upset, talking so loud and fast that I couldn't understand her. She handed the phone to a young man whom I knew well, demanding that I "talk to him!" He had just returned from a stint in rehab and was ready to get back to work. I asked why she was upset, and he responded in his slow drawl, "Well, I missed showers this morning, so I was here in the bathroom washing myself up when she opened the door and started screaming. I tried to cover up with paper towels but everybody in the building ran in to see why she was screaming. She held the door wide open and pointed at me, saying I was *masturbating in the bathroom.* Now, I wasn't, but I did ask her where a better place to do that might be."

I could picture his sly teasing grin and had to take a long pause. When I could talk without laughing, I suggested he lock the door the next time he used the bathroom. He gave her back the phone and I reminded her that people expect privacy in the bathroom. I asked her not to open the door without first knocking. We never discussed it again but she gave him a fierce *stink eye* whenever they were in the same room. He always winked back.

I am glad to be reminded of how humor also swirled through the center at unexpected times. I was working late one evening, trying to meet the deadline for a grant, when someone knocked rapidly on my window. We were closed and my blinds were down, so I tried to ignore it. When the knocking persisted, I cracked the blind to find a familiar face looking at me with a frantic expression. It seemed urgent, so I walked around and opened the door. Looking furtively over his shoulder, he lowered his voice and leaned in to ask softly, "Do you have any of them

'Crack Cookies?" This was a craving I understood. He wanted almond praline cookies. These were an exquisite concoction of chopped almonds mixed with a brown sugar and butter toffee, baked until crisp, then dipped in dark chocolate. A fledgling company had created these unbelievably delicious cookies and were still perfecting their craft during that time. They would cull 'imperfect' cookies with irregular shapes, or 'too much chocolate." I still have difficulty comprehending that this is a real thing. Rather than throwing these out, they generously tossed them into huge plastic bags and donated them to the center's nutrition program. For many months before they achieved uniformity, imperfect cookies were offered for dessert at daily lunches, added to volunteer take-home meals, and distributed in weekly food boxes. They were so abundant that I also took them to meetings and shared them with other agencies. I like to believe that I contributed to that company's great success by helping the entire community to become hooked. The first ones were free.

On this night, I asked him to wait, carefully closed the door and walked back into my office. I closed the blinds again and opened the bottom drawer of my desk to retrieve a baggie containing 6 cookies. They were passed through the crack in the door with a strong warning, "If you tell anyone where you got these, I will deny it." He nodded in fervent agreement before running back into the darkness.

There was also real danger and I sometimes missed warnings. I quickly learned not to approach anyone who was overly paranoid. There also was one middle-aged man who came in for services and stayed to become one of our most dependable volunteers for a very long time. His outward appearance displayed piercings and scary tattoos that covered his entire body like armor that seemed to protect the kind and gentle spirit beneath. He also flashed a beautiful smile while working and giving everything he had, to whatever he did. I knew that he dealt with a serious mental illness only because he told me so. Taking full responsibility for managing his illness, it wasn't obvious to anyone who didn't know him. He would walk an hour to arrive before 7 AM every morning, rain, or shine, and carry a bag of trash from his own secret squat (camp) that was hidden up in the forest. He would do anything that we needed, stocking, mopping, sweeping, cleaning bathrooms, doing laundry, or picking up litter. Every few months, he would disappear for a day or two, but always came back. Then one day, I stepped out a side door to find him sitting against the back fence. He was curled up with his arms over his head and rocking back and forth as if in pain. I rushed over to ask what I could do but he seemed not to hear me. Just as I reached out to touch his shoulder, he quietly said, "You need to leave." I went back inside and periodically checked to see how he was doing. I didn't see him go, but at some point, he was gone. He didn't return the next day, or the next. On the fourth day, I received a call from a doctor in a city several hundred miles away, who informed me that our friend would not be returning. He had given permission to tell me and to thank me and others at the center. I later heard that he walked many miles in the night and then took a bus to voluntarily commit himself. His "demon voices" had come back and were telling him to do terrible things. He was one of the most interesting, intelligent, and responsible people I have ever encountered. We missed him. Another true hero who refuses to surrender to an enemy few of us can imagine.

People who frequented the center were flawed and beautiful human beings just like the rest of us. Whatever food or material assistance they accepted, it was the nourishment that came from having a community that they most required, even if only briefly. This seemed also to be true for those who sat silently in a corner.

I understood that the town would one day have to decide whether they wanted this program to remain in their community. I hoped the newspaper articles would help guide that decision.

The building was located very close to downtown and the

term 'perfect storm' still comes to mind. If you build it, they *will* come. And they will be especially visible. It is difficult to ignore this desperate situation when confronted by it every day. We want them to go away but instead their numbers grow.

The center was also close to a university whose students sometimes displayed many of the same behaviors (public intoxication, drug use, alley urination, and noisy disturbances that included profanity and fights). Students are better tolerated because they represent the possibility of success rather than failure. They are also a source of dependable revenue.

One early morning before work, you and I were having a rare breakfast together downtown. We had a window seat and watched a young couple crawl out of a BMW with university tags. They had parked in front of the coffee shop where we were enjoying exquisite pastries and expensive espresso coffees, which were a treat for us. As they started into the shop, they caught sight of two volunteers from the center, a young married couple with blond dreadlocks, who were pushing the center's clean-up cart through downtown and filling it with trash from the night before. The students stopped and pointed, laughing while one shouted, "Look! The trash is picking up the trash." I gazed into your eyes and asked, "Which couple do you think should reproduce?" You spat your coffee back into your cup so you wouldn't choke on it.

During my third year at the center, I experienced an adversarial relationship with a woman who considered herself a leader in the houseless community. She wanted to bring pride to street people and was one of several who promoted "free living." They encouraged people to call themselves 'Frees' rather than 'Homeless', 'Houseless' or `Unsheltered' and believed in being free from the constraints of mainstream mandates. There is pride in choice.

It is true that many people can easily live off the waste the rest of us create and a legitimate case was frequently made that people who were free from driving cars, or shopping, created less waste, fewer toxins, and did much less environmental damage overall than "mainstream robots". Some people do choose this as an alternate lifestyle but most strive to also be safe and out of the weather.

Unfortunately, the environmental damage that was occurring because of illegal camping and drug use was more locally visible. As numbers increased, 'free people' took over parks and natural areas that were meant to be shared with others, including wild animals and birds. Forests, streams, and marsh areas became trampled and filled with dog and human waste, needles, and drug paraphernalia. Self-policing was helpful, but the problem grew too large with too many newcomers in the mix. There were few alternatives besides jail, which was costly and did nothing to solve the problem long term.

One day I invited a group of partner agency heads to experience a typical meal of mostly outdated but still safe and highly nutritional foods that were destined for the land fill, or pig farmers. This advocate for the 'Frees' became outraged that any of "our food" would go to "them," forgetting where it had originated. She came shouting and threatening into my office and was forced to leave. When she was told not to return, it became personal. This is how I acquired my very first nemesis. We should all experience one. Every time I was confronted by her, I met myself. My own weakness, prejudice, and unacknowledged anger often surfaced as I was forced to deal with unexamined feelings of inadequacy, frustration, and distrust.

Advocates and leaders from the homeless community often made good points, especially when advocating for the very human need of a place to sleep or use the bathroom. However, when it became necessary for Nemesis to hold a rational discussion about how some of the problems might be resolved, she went off the rails and was unable to climb back on. She attended City

Council meetings and demanded things on behalf of the Free community without also acknowledging that taxes and donations from working people paid for the building that we were using, not to mention the parks, streets, sidewalks, etc. Working people generously shared their personal resources with us, while local businesses and grocery stores donated huge amounts of food and supplies. Rather than bringing people together, she had difficulty reconciling in her mind that if everyone lived *free*, the community that supports us all would collapse. It is not possible for housed or unhoused folks to separate themselves from each other. We are us.

The city was swamped with complaints and sponsored a meeting with community members and downtown business owners, encouraging them to voice their concerns and the problem of falling sales that were blamed on clients of the center, who congregated in the downtown area near the center. The Chief of Police invited me to share the podium and help to respond to complaints, explain laws and limitations, and explore possible solutions. I walked with a board member, who was also a friend, to the hotel where the meeting was taking place. As we approached the main entrance, we were confronted by three protesters led by Nemesis, who was still upset about the luncheon and about being banned. She wanted revenge. They were carrying signs that read, *"Fire Sandi Paris!"* When my friend saw this, she turned on her heel to head the other way, but I hooked her elbow with mine and pulled her along with me. As we got closer, one of the protestors called out, "We love you, Sandi!" Nemesis scowled. I smiled and asked, "So, what are you doing?" He confessed "She gave us new socks." This was a valuable commodity. I asked if anyone wanted to come into the meeting, offering to arrange it if they promised not to create a disturbance. I believe they learned by hearing other perspectives and gave balance to the conversations, particularly when responding to some questions from the business community. I wished I'd invited them earlier.

Tension was high and the room was packed with business and

restaurant owners, shop keepers, and residential neighbors of the downtown area. As I looked around, I saw a few friendly faces and then spotted *you*. You were sitting toward the back, watching me. When you caught my eye, you smiled and gave a wink. I had no idea you had planned to take time off work to be there. You knew it would be a stressful event, but you didn't know you would have to walk past protest signs calling for my removal. You were as solidly with me as ever.

We asked people sitting in each row to introduce themselves and when it was your turn, you stood up and said, "My name is Randy Brown and I'm the *lucky man* who is married to Sandi Paris." People smiled and chuckled. I thought nothing bad could ever happen to me again.

A day later, I was in the garden pushing myself into a physical frenzy, cutting flowers, dragging hoses, and running up and down our hill like a maniac after cleaning house and baking a birthday cake to celebrate a friend's 50th birthday that evening. I gradually realized that I couldn't breathe properly and passed out. You had taken Jordan out of town to look at colleges and I was alone. I eventually crawled up to the house, lying flat whenever I felt dizzy and managed to take a shower (because that's what everyone does when they might be dying). I was lying on the stairs when my friend, a nurse, arrived early. She helped me to the couch until her MD husband showed up and made the decision to drive me the short distance to the emergency room where a blood test confirmed elevated Troponin levels, which indicated muscle damage from a heart event. They transported me by ambulance to the cardiac unit in a nearby town where I spent three days in step-down intensive care. My heart stabilized and I was discharged without a clear diagnosis. There was no arterial blockage, and it remained a mystery until five years later when I had another serious event while skiing. It was finally diagnosed as an unusual cardiomyopathy (Takotsubo) nicknamed the

Broken Heart Syndrome because it is usually triggered by a sudden emotional shock, like an earthquake, or when a mother drops dead after hearing that her child has died in a tragic accident. Mine was triggered by physical activity. I didn't fit into anyone's tidy diagnosis box but was warned to manage my stress level anyway. It can be life threatening.

We were both somber after leaving the hospital that first time. You started the car and then paused to look over at me with a teasing smile. My conservative brother had once declared that he had finally figured out what 'the problem' with me was. You parroted him by saying, "Well, you *look* normal!" Laughter took us home again.

After the first heart event the doctors ordered me to take time off work and I never returned full time. You kept encouraging me to resign. I finally did a few months later, after you stridently pointed out that a fully trained staff was in place, along with funding that would carry them for another two years. Once again, you held a door open for me by pointing out what seemed like a good time to make a change. The town would eventually decide that the center should be somewhere else.

Just weeks after I resigned, you and your sister, Terri, were forced to make an emergency trip to rescue your mother, Patricia, who lived in Arizona. She was in an early stage of Alzheimer's dementia and being financially abused and physically neglected by a caregiver. You would discover that Pat's bank accounts had been drained, most of her retirement income was spent within hours of deposit and her credit cards were maxed. Worse, they had coerced her into signing papers to refinance the family home and liquidate the equity. When asked about it, she had no idea any of this had happened. The money was gone and payments were never made on the new loan. It took over a year for the bank to foreclose, and then evict.

You and Terri had both been having trouble reaching her by

telephone and left many messages. One day, Terri received a call from neighbors that there was a foreclosure notice on the door and a U-Haul truck in the driveway. The neighbor followed the U-Haul to a location a few miles away and wrote down the address, which she gave to Terri. You and Terri coordinated flights, rented a car, and drove there together. It was 105 degrees in Arizona when you arrived at the rental house to find your elderly mother standing alone in the middle of a strange yard. You described her wringing her hands and turning around in circles until she recognized you walking toward her and began to sob. You called me that evening to ask if I would consider caring for her while you sorted things out. Terri was working full-time and still raising children. I was the only one available to do this. I said, "Of course. Bring her home."

Her appearance shocked me when she arrived. She was thin, nearly bald, and walked with a slow shuffle. She had not showered for some time. I immediately got her to a doctor who found that she was dehydrated and had a raging urinary tract infection. In addition, her thyroid and cholesterol medications had not been filled. Lab work showed thyroid levels were undetectable, while cholesterol was dangerously high after having had a stroke the year before. These were serious and life-threatening medical conditions.

After talking with an attorney, you and Terri decided *not* to file criminal charges for elder abuse. It would have required considerable time and additional expense to travel back and forth between states, which would take each of you away from your own jobs and families. Nor would incarceration have restored the funds that would have provided better choices for Patricia's care. You also knew that prison rarely rehabilitates offenders. Particularly in Arizona. We still endured several years of creditors calling for Pat, even after hiring an attorney to establish Identity Theft. In the end, she was safe and content.

I spent nearly a year nursing myself and Pat back to health. She was socially engaged and as medication and nutrition corrected her chemistry, her hair grew back and her body filled out. She would eventually walk up our steep hill every day to get the mail. Her short-term memory loss continued to worsen but she was engaged with life again. I loved making her laugh. In time, we found an assisted living home nearby so I could return to work. You never took my efforts for granted and repeatedly thanked me for welcoming and caring for your mom.

My new job was unrelated to homelessness or poverty. Everyone I worked with had adequate income, health insurance, and housing. I learned much and enjoyed my years as a medical social worker, but lessons from the center were life changing.

Without time spent at there, I would not have witnessed the humanity hidden beneath the stench, trauma, and illness. I could not understand how it could be more terrifying to let go of a destructive way of life that is familiar, than to reach for a new life that cannot be imagined. Opportunity only exists for those who recognize it.

I learned to recognize hopelessness hiding in plain sight. It is held up in shameful signs and in hands stretching out with palms turned up. It rides on the loud demands and exploding anger that we all resent. Hopelessness encourages someone to spend their last $5 on cigarettes rather than food, because that moment of feeling good is as far as they can see. This awareness is not meant to excuse abhorrent behaviors but to acknowledge them. They are *canaries in the coal mine* and a warning to us all.

We have never seen a pattern of homelessness like we do now. Historically, high numbers of homeless have appeared for brief periods after wars, industrial and other disruptions like the Dust Bowl, or stock market and housing crashes. When the country recovered, homeless people also recovered. Aside from that very small percentage of mostly alcoholic men who lived under bridges or in old hotels and boarding houses, we have never seen people on the streets like we do now. Instead of following the larger economy when it improves, homeless rates have not decreased but continued to rise over recent years.

Our resistance to giving someone something they haven't 'earned' is at the core of our American identity, but we are only able to cling to the myth of "self-made" by ignoring uncomfortable truths.

We all know people who work hard and sincerely believe they live a comfortable life *because* they work hard. There is no doubt that hard work contributes, but it is critical to acknowledge that many people work just as hard, or harder, for wages that do not cover their basic needs. Some have difficulty finding full time work and must juggle multiple part-time jobs. Still others barely work at all and yet generate tremendous wealth, sometimes on the backs of these other people. It is difficult to reconcile this with the growing public health crisis of homelessness that is now visible everywhere we go. It can no longer be explained away by 'poor choices.'

In the 50s and 60s, mental hospitals were mostly dismantled so patients could return to their communities and be treated by state programs that were never fully funded. Many of these people became part of this new chronically homeless population. More recently, addiction rates soared during the opioid epidemic and sent more people into the streets, or to jail, which also leads to homelessness when job and housing opportunities become even more inaccessible to people with a record of incarceration. They are still disproportionately people of color.

Much of the distain and hatred felt for homeless people is fear based. They represent something we are frightened of: *Failure.* Not theirs, but the possibility of our own. If this can happen to them, we know at some deep level that it can happen to us. It is terrifying to consider that the unwashed person who is panhandling on a street corner may be as deserving as we are.

You once commented that it was, "sobering" when you realized that your own success wasn't just because of hard work and "good choices." You worked hard, but also made more than a few bad choices. Your family and community were your safety net. They instilled confidence by letting you know that you were valuable. As a young man, it was natural to reach for what you believed you deserved. You also came to understand that maleness and stature and whiteness and intelligence had cleared obstacles from your path. And your college education did not leave you with a mountain of debt. Belief in yourself was reinforced by hands that stretched out and doors that unlocked for you, but not for others.

Certain politicians say the word "entitlement" like it is profane, particularly when directed at programs that support low and middle-income people. This word becomes truly profane when distorted by the very people who feel entitled to redistribute our shared resources and create wealth for themselves and their constituents, while defunding and weakening the public institutions that protect us. *It tells a different story about who is receiving something they haven't earned.*

Both of my working-class parents expressed outrage that immigrants and black people were trying to "take over." They were fearful that there would be more of 'them' and fewer of 'us' and they would get *for free* what we have worked so hard for. They forgot whose land their home was erected on and whose backs were harnessed to build the foundation of this country we are so proud of. They worked hard too.

My mother was quite elderly when she looked straight at me and declared that "if the 'do-gooders' would quit feeding 'those people' they would go away." When I asked where they might go, she said "somewhere else." Mother needed to forget the alcoholism, misogyny, violence, and poverty her family suffered when she was a child. And she most needed to forget the handouts and assistance from church and family that kept them from the streets. She needed to *not* remember how her minimum wage paid for basic housing, transportation, and food. She chose not to recall the free childcare and public education, and not worrying about huge insurance or medical bills. And then, when she married my dad, she knew they would be able to buy a house and live comfortably on his modest wage, without her having to work outside the home. It used to be that way for some folks. It was never that way for others and those numbers are growing.

Wages once kept pace with inflation and our tax dollars once funded childcare and education. *What changed?* We know that other developed and democratic countries provide trade and college education, and better medical care to all their citizens, at a lower cost. *Why can't we?* We also know that other, less wealthy, countries consider housing to be a basic human right. *Why don't we?*

One thing is abundantly clear: An extraordinary number of people are homeless because we, as a nation, allow them to be. It is difficult for most of us to wrap our heads around the obscene amounts of money that some wealthy individuals and large corporations spend to pay lobbyist and support those representatives (on both sides of the isle) who are willing to weaken regulations that protect public and environmental health, to make sure their already staggering profits are not reduced. They also pay billions of dollars for advertising and media messaging that tell people, like my mother, how 'entitlements' come out of their pockets and reward laziness. Corporations are not evil. They are doing what they are designed to do.

We do not have a problem with *government*. We have a problem with voters who are asleep at the wheel. American people aren't stupid, we just aren't seeking the valid information we need to make informed decisions and direct our representatives to fight for the people without money and power, who also need access to them. Voters allowed Citizens United to pass (2010), giving corporations increased influence over our elections and our constitutional rights. Reversing this would be a good place to start.

The promise of a civilized Democratic society seems to be sliding back down the hill it has been struggling up for hundreds of years. Extreme wealth is promoted as a God-given virtue, despite the social and economic struggles of workers and consumers who help create it. Rome didn't fall in a day, but it did fall. We could rewrite this story if we wanted to.

Here I am all charged up and ranting to myself again. I want to hear your sweet voice chuckling and saying, "Settle down now..."

Unimaginable

I'M NOT YOUR fucking mother! We were both stunned when those words came out of my mouth. Neither of us was opposed to using the F-word for emphasis on occasion. We did not attack each other with it, or with anything else.

Your eyes widened and you froze as I tried to get control of my anger. After a year or two of stepping up to do things that you had stepped back from, a full garbage can was the tipping point. I watched you lay trash on the counter above the overflowing compactor, and then walk away. I didn't recognize that my burning rage was being fueled by fear.

You were still immobilized when I said more calmly, "We agreed that if either of us becomes unhappy, we would talk about it and decide the best way forward." When you didn't respond, I continued, "It's clear to me that you are unhappy, either with me (where many women go first) or with your life in general. Whatever it is, you need to decide what you want to do about it. I am telling you right now that I will NOT beg you to take out the damn garbage! For god's sake, it's one of the few things in this house you are still responsible for. The laundry is done, the house is clean, the garden is managed, and I purchase and cook most of the food. Have you forgotten that I work too? You are no longer interested in my thoughts and you don't share much about yours when I ask. You haven't cooked for weeks, and you act surprised when it's time to go somewhere that we've planned. I am not going to oversee putting things on your damn calendar either."

I realized I had been angry for a long while. I remember how good it felt to unleash my frustration and how hard it was to stop. As I spewed the last of my venom in your direction, I ended with, "This is not the relationship we had. If it is what you want now, I will leave you."

In retrospect, I am unsure which words you absorbed. There is no doubt that you soaked up every bit of my anger and disappointment. You remained frozen, like a trapped animal knowing it should run but unable to move. When I allowed silence to finally settle into the space between us, your eyes filled with tears and you put your hands up to both sides of your head, rubbing, like it hurt. I watched you do this strange thing until you finally said, "I don't know what you are talking about," and began to sob. You sobbed from the deepest part of your soul, like a tortured child. You were as sincere and vulnerable as I had ever seen you. I believed you. You had no idea what I was talking about or why I was upset.

I wrapped my arms around you and whispered over and over that we would "figure it out." I knew in that moment that your inattention was not deliberate. It was true that your work had been unusually stressful, which was why I had been so willing to step up. You promised to try and do better. I promised to let you know when I needed something specific from you. Deep down, I knew that 'work stress' explanations had gone on for too long, but I wanted to be comforted too. Over the next few days, when things were calmer, I tried pointing out changes you seemed unaware of:

- You used to calmly pull over on mountain roads to let aggressive drivers pass, but now you raged. Rather than saying, "You just want to let those guys go by," you sped up and shouted, "That guy is on my ass!" You seemed not to comprehend the difference when I pointed it out to you.
- You often insisted that I hadn't told you something we previously discussed. I began to interpret this as disinterest. Instead of admitting that you hadn't understood, or had forgotten, you kept saying I definitely "hadn't told you",

or that I had "used the wrong words." Another clue to language loss I missed.

- Sometimes you would come home shaking your head after a meeting and say, "Those young biologists aren't making any sense. I can hardly understand them." You used sophisticated nouns like *verbiage* but couldn't name the person who had spoken. I thought it was a generational thing. Neither of us thought it was atrophy in the language center of your brain.

- You used to recycle, take out garbage, cook, and do house maintenance without being asked. You would jump up to help make the bed when I pulled sheets out of the dryer and now seemed either unaware or unsure of what needed to be done.

- You became disorganized and couldn't find things in the garage or your office. You compensated by running out and purchasing more tools, hardware, supplies, and storage containers.

These conversations went nowhere. You listened carefully but had little insight and would shake your head, saying "I don't know." At one point you suggested that I was "fabricating" things. I began to wonder if anyone else observed what I was seeing. I asked your son, Jordan, if he noticed anything different about you. He laughed and said, "No. Dad's always been weird." Years later, he admitted that it drove him crazy when you would call him and then play solitaire or read things to him off the computer while he was on the phone. It was a long time before we realized you wanted to hear his voice but could no longer have a meaningful conversation.

I met with your close friend and co-worker, Paula, to ask if she had noticed anything at work. She said you seemed stressed and distracted, but fine overall. She confirmed that things were difficult at the office and saw it as a stress response to that. She didn't think it was anything to worry about.

I eventually talked you into seeing the doctor, just to rule out anything physical. When the nurse asked why the doctor was seeing you that day, you looked toward me quizzically and said, "The ringing in my ears?" When I shook my head, you thought for a moment and then joked, "Oh! I can't remember shit!" Of course, we laughed. The doctor came in and gave you a quick once-over, then did a mini-mental health test which you passed with flying colors. You were time/day oriented, knew who the president was, could draw a clock, and recalled the 3 simple words you were asked you to remember. He reassured us that you were likely just stressed and that worry would only make it worse. He prescribed an antidepressant and suggested that I was overreacting because of your mother's Alzheimer-type dementia. I tried to feel encouraged rather than offended.

A few months after this, your mother's second assisted living facility announced it was closing. When my work also announced it was downsizing and eliminating my position, we decided I would retire early and bring her home to live with us again. By then, she was in mid-stage dementia. Since I seemed to be the only one concerned about you, I began to focus on the house and garden, and keeping Patricia safe and happy. I tried to ignore the worry that kept creeping into my mind.

After my meltdown, you seemed more responsive when asked to help with something, but you rarely initiated. I noticed you had to be *shown* rather than *told* things.

More than once, you paid the same bill twice, while neglecting another that went past due. Unlike most of us who just use a checkbook register, you had a spreadsheet to track expenses. Mistakes like that had never happened before.

You became less interactive when we socialized. One night we invited friends over for dinner and you seemed disinterested, contributing little to the conversation. We were still eating when you left the table, so I assumed you had gone to the bathroom. You never returned. I found you in your study playing solitaire on the computer. This behavior became more frequent and I found myself making excuses for you. I tried not to feel resentment because you were still so stressed, and now your mother Pat was living with us. I ignored my gut again.

One day, Paula called to ask if she could stop by on her way home from work and share a glass of wine in the garden. It had been more than a year since our first conversation. When we sat on a bench near the pond, she gently said that things at work hadn't improved and were much worse. Staff was starting to complain and everyone was becoming frustrated and concerned. We both had tears in our eyes when she finished.

I made another doctor's appointment and this time he ordered some lab work. While we were waiting for the appointment, the doctor called. He was excited to say that the labs indicated a very low B12, which he believed might explain your symptoms. He thought it was reversible. I felt some of my tension lift but noticed that you were curiously indifferent. You immediately started on B12 therapy. Then, while we were waiting for improvement, three things happened in quick succession over just a few weeks. Like the snowball that gets bigger as it rolls down the mountain, something larger and more dangerous was coming our way.

Event #1 - I had prepared a closing statement for our tenants who had moved and asked you to look it over for accuracy. You suggested inserting a comma somewhere before handing it back, saying, "Looks OK." I tried to engage you about content. "Did I convey my appreciation for them in spite of the charges?" You said you couldn't *speak to that.* I then asked if I could borrow your calculator to check my numbers one last time. You looked confused, "What?" I repeated, "Calculator." You said, "Is it this?" and tried to hand me a stapler. As I reached for the calculator on the shelf just above your head, you grabbed it out of my hand

and inspected it suspiciously. Turning it over and over you asked, "Where does it say calculator?"

Event #2 - I went to the store, loaded groceries into the back of my car and closed it, locking my bag with keys and cell phone inside. I borrowed a cell phone from a nice man in the parking lot and called you. I knew you had a light day at work and were only 10 minutes from home. I offered to buy you lunch if you would run over and pick up the extra set of keys. You became agitated, saying you needed to complete something important but the "computer was messing up" and you had a "deadline." I knew this was an annual report that you usually knocked out in less than an hour, but said, "OK, no worries. I'll just call our insurance and have them send someone to open the car." You raised your voice, declaring, **"No! That won't work."** I reassured you that it would, but you became more upset and shouted, **"I'm coming!"** Then hung up on me. I gave back the phone I had borrowed and waited. An hour and a half later, you arrived with a bag of keys. You had house keys, pad lock keys, a shed key, car rack keys, toolbox keys, and a key to the safe. You did not have my car keys. I tried to stop you from inserting these keys into the car locks, but you persisted, sticking each one in and then going to the next, getting more frustrated and perplexed with each failure. I finally put my hand over yours and asked if I could borrow your phone. You surrendered it to me and then watched very intently as I called our insurance and arranged for someone to come out. You were silent.

Event #3 - The very next day was a holiday and you were home with your mom so I could catch up on errands. On my way home, I called to ask if you would put on a pot of water for pasta, which was our version of 'fast food'. You asked, "What pot?" I said, "You know, the BIG pot that we use to cook spaghetti." You asked, "Where is it?" I responded, "With the pots and pans, next to the stove." You asked, "What?" I repeated, "The cabinet next to the stove." You wouldn't let me hang up, asking, "What should I do?" I responded impatiently, "How about you fill it with WATER and turn on the gas?" And then you paused before asking softly, *"What's water?"* The frustration I felt was replaced with a sharp terror. This wasn't just a B12 deficiency. Something was terribly wrong.

When I calmly suggested that you order pizza, the relief in your "OK" was deafening. For months you had been ordering pizza on your nights to cook. You had our favorite pizza parlor on speed dial and would order the same pizza every time.

That evening I shot an email off to the doctor, describing each event. The next day I babbled on the phone, saying it was "probably a tumor since your actual memory seemed sort of OK because you didn't repeat yourself or get lost like your mom but you seemed confused and had trouble understanding random things and your personality had changed and..." The doctor gently stopped me. "Let's find out." He ordered an MRI of your brain.

After this first MRI, the doctor called us in to share the results. He was grim. The radiologist report indicated atrophy, primarily in the tissue of your left temporal lobe. He said it looked like early Alzheimer's disease. By then, you were 51 years old. Alzheimer's most commonly affects people over the age of 65. The doctor referred you to a local Neurologist who agreed with the diagnosis and then provided us with literature and contact numbers for support groups. She started you on an Alzheimer's medication that "might help a little" but advised us to prepare for the "inevitable decline."

Your work agreed to accommodate you while we figured things out and I began reading everything I could about alternative treatments. I changed your diet and began adding coconut oil to everything you ate. You continued to work with less responsibility, while I kept you active and socially connected. I could not see the most common symptoms of Alzheimer's. There was still no short-term memory loss, you didn't repeat yourself, you didn't misplace your coat, keys, or get lost in familiar places. You seemed to forget things we *talked* about and had trouble communicating effectively. You couldn't always identify or name common items and had become strangely disorganized. You would mix up the steps for certain activities like building a fire, cooking a meal, starting laundry. You got confused about what to do and when to do things and had increasing difficulty following instructions or problem solving. You became emotionally detached and more agitated.

A few months after this first diagnosis, your supervisor suggested getting you to an urban medical center for a second opinion. We both felt the diagnosis wasn't right and I requested referral to a neurological center in San Francisco. It took months to get an appointment and more months of testing and imaging to receive an accurate diagnosis. They eventually changed your diagnosis from Early-Onset Alzheimer's to Semantic Dementia, a variant of Frontotemporal Deterioration (svFTD) with Primary Progressive Aphasia (PPM). A light was shining at the end of our tunnel and it was definitely a train.

They invited you to enter a long-term study which would contribute to identifying causes and potential treatments for FTD. You were still a scientist and said that you wanted to contribute to their research. You didn't seem to absorb that you had just been diagnosed with a terminal illness, nor did you recognize that it had already taken away much of the person you used to be.

As I began figuring out how to navigate this new terrain, I knew that your disability accommodation at work could not continue much longer. I worked with the doctor and your supervisor, who lobbied with upper management to use your accumulated sick leave with monthly updates, which give us more time. I read that most people lose their jobs before they are accurately diagnosed. Marriages disintegrate, savings accounts are depleted, and homes are repossessed before anyone understands what is happening. You were fortunate to have the supervisor you did, as she worked very hard to accommodate you for as long as possible. I heard her tell someone on the phone, "He has worked for us for thirty years and we need to do this right."

When I learned that it also took many months, sometimes years, to apply for and receive disability status, I got busy. Even with disability, our income would be a fraction of what it had been. While you finished up your remaining sick leave, I navigated the complex applications and documentation required from Social Security Disability Insurance (SSDI). It took months, but not years. A special category for illnesses like yours allowed your application to be expedited, which then allowed me to help you also apply for disability retirement through your work. As our income fell, we spent down our savings, but felt fortunate to even have savings. When savings were gone, we began drawing on investment funds. The initial goal was to keep our home and somehow keep you there with me. I began to hope that you, the man who didn't own a TV when I met him, would eventually surrender to one. I wanted the sounds and images moving across the screen to anesthetize your anxious mind and become all you needed from life. It was shameful of me, but your retirement gift was a large screen TV and a stack of favorite movies. This was safe.

Once you were at home full time, I contacted your sister Terri in Texas to ask if she could take your mother and care for her or place her nearby. It was a difficult thing to do but I knew I couldn't manage both of you.

Your behavior toward you mother had become mean spirited. You would roll your eyes and chastise her when she didn't remember things (she was the only one with *short-term* memory loss). You would also scoff or correct her in an unkind tone when she mixed things up, remembered something incorrectly, or dwelled on a childhood that she could still describe with fascinating detail. She couldn't remember your own childhood or the day you were born, which angered you.

One day I was outside in the garden, when I heard loud voices in the house. I ran upstairs to find you standing over your mother, who was sitting in front of the TV. You had the TV remote in your hand and were holding it up out of her reach while she tried to pull your arm down, demanding, "Give that back!" It was shocking. I intervened "What is happening here?" You shouted in outrage, "SHE was watching FOX NEWS. WE don't watch FOX NEWS." At that point, Pat got up and furiously stomped upstairs to her bedroom. Her slamming door rattled the windows. It was like having adolescents in the house again but without the comfort of knowing that they would eventually mature and learn to manage themselves better.

This was not going to get easier and there was no way to reason with you. I followed Pat upstairs a few minutes later and found her sitting in her rocking chair with a book in her lap. She was looking peacefully out her window at the forest. When I asked if she wanted to watch her news program on the TV in her room, she looked surprised and then smiled sweetly and explained, "I'm reading my book," tenderly holding up a copy of *Listening Woman*, by Tony Hillerman. I knew she read the same pages over and over. The book she held was one of several books she picked out repeatedly from our local thrift store. It was an outing she enjoyed and when she accumulated too many duplicates, I would donate them back. We would then go treasure hunting again and she would be delighted to find her favorite books once more. I sometimes had to sneak into her room to reclaim my own books, so she could borrow them again. Now, she was happy with her book and had already forgotten the angry outburst from her son that had sent her fleeing upstairs. This was a sweet benefit of short-term memory loss.

A few months after Pat was settled with Terri and her family, we visited them during a month-long trip of driving across the country together. She had already forgotten our home and her years with us. This would be our last time with her. It was reassuring to see how content she was with Terri and her husband, Rusty. During the remainder of that trip, we saw our spectacular country with fresh eyes and visited friends and family along the way. It was a memorable and exhausting journey. I did all the driving and managed your unpredictable behaviors in unfamiliar places. If we had waited even two months longer, I would have had to turn around. Your disease was quickly progressing, and it was becoming more difficult to keep you safe and content.

The morning after we returned home, I discovered you could no longer make coffee. For many years before this trip, you had ground fresh beans and made the perfect cup of coffee every morning before delivering it upstairs to me, with a kiss. I let myself expect that this one simple thing might continue forever. I was *desperate* for it to continue. When it became clear I couldn't re-teach you how to grind and measure, I bought a coffee maker with those little plastic capsules that are expensive and wasteful, justifying that it would be easier for you. You managed the capsules but then filled the water container with milk and ruined the machine. I bought another one. After a week of careful training, you did the same thing. I locked the bathroom door and sobbed wretchedly. The world had ended. Again.

When I opened the bathroom door, I said a firm goodbye to your alter ego, Naked Kitchen Man, who used to cook and make coffee in the nude (except for an occasional apron), which I always found to be hilariously dangerous. I accepted that clothed or unclothed, these were things you would no longer do. It was the worst I would allow myself to imagine at that time.

Last Times

A NOTABLE THING about last times is that we are so often unaware they are happening. Every morning someone, somewhere, wakes up to find a loved one gone. People walk away or die without permission. Whether they go suddenly or slowly, it is when we look back that we realize, oh, that was the last time we did that; went there; made love; laughed; fought; danced; or said I love you.

With your dementia diagnosis we were given time which proved to be a very lonely process for the only one who was aware of our long goodbye. It was strangely comforting when you were eventually unable to understand what was happening to you. There was no comfort when you forgot our life together. In between this living and dying, there were also many decisions to be made. It is a monstrous responsibility.

I felt a huge sense of relief when you voluntarily stopped doing a thing that had become unsafe. I liked not having to make the decision for you. But once I knew in the pit of my gut that something you still enjoyed must end, I would carefully consider the urgency and weigh whether to exert full control or more slowly manipulate you into letting it go. It was agonizing. I would repeatedly ask myself: When does safety become the most important thing for someone with a terminal diagnosis? How can anyone be sure when it is the 'right time' to take something away from another person? Exactly how much should other people's discomfort be allowed to limit the freedom of someone who can't understand that they are behaving badly? Is it ever appropriate to blatantly lie to a person who cannot reason? The answers were all the same: *It depends.*

I began to feel like Alice falling down that Rabbit Hole. I could not have predicted how quickly the world would reshape

117

itself. Everything seemed out of place or unfamiliar, and danger lurked around every corner. The way forward was often unclear unless you somehow let me know that it was time to let go.

Last time behind the wheel

We called your compact 4-Wheel drive pickup the "car truck" because of the back seat. You could carry passengers and go to recycle, or haul yard debris, or toss your bicycle and snowboards in the back and be off for a weekend of adventure. You loved that truck.

I remember that one of the early tests of relationship compatibility was watching how you behaved behind the wheel. I was in an earlier relationship with a man who was gentle and compassionate while his feet were touching the ground. He became a wild and aggressive asshole when he had wheels under him. He would honk and pass on blind corners, tail gate little old ladies on mountain roads, and speed up in snowy conditions to slide around the people who had slowed down. When he got out of the car, he became normal again while his passengers kissed the ground and headed for the nearest bar. You passed that test with high marks. You had always been a skilled, considerate, and cautious driver. When that changed, it also became clear to me that you would not give up driving without a struggle. Driving, especially in our culture, is a considerable source of pride and independence.

After your diagnosis you were automatically banned from driving work vehicles, because of the liability. The day they notified you, you came home angry and mortified. I had the same concern about liability as they did but could not reason with you. I took it slow and watched carefully. You still knew your way around town and seemed to understand basic rules of the road. You drove the short distance back and forth to work, for months without incident. One day, I was a passenger while you were driving, and we came to a detour sign because of road work. You ignored it and drove through the traffic cones to continue the route you were used to taking. Of course, there were frantic waving arms outside and shouts of alarm inside (mine). I convinced you to stop, but not without considerable effort. When we got home, I hid the truck keys and contacted your neurologist. She worked you in the following day and explained to you that she had neglected to notify DMV of your diagnosis, which is a requirement. She told you they probably wouldn't allow you to drive any longer. You were very upset. She said you could request a review after you received the notice in the mail. As you angrily talked about "bad" DMV, she and I locked eyes while voicing agreement that you had the right to challenge them. I understood that she knew what I knew: *You would be unable to navigate the appeal process on your own.*

I became very busy while you struggled with the paperwork until the deadline passed. Then, after numerous searches that I pretended to participate in, your truck keys were never found. You finally quit looking for them. I knew I had waited too long to take this action, which put others at risk. Someone could have been injured. I promised myself that I would become more watchful and more manipulative as things progressed.

The truck sat in the driveway for nearly a year until you didn't seem to notice it anymore. I decided it was time to sell. When the people came to pick it up, I arranged for you to be somewhere else and somberly watched it roll up the driveway until the taillights disappeared. Less than an hour later, you walked out to the front deck and looked down at the driveway. You pointed at the empty spot where your truck had been and asked, "Is that not there now?" I shook my head sadly, confirming "Not there." You walked back into the house. You did the same thing the next day, pointed and asked, "Is that not there now?" That was it. You never asked again.

Unfortunately, you replaced driving with navigating and became the 'Navigator from Hell.' You shouted, "STOP!" at every stop sign or red light. You would also yell "GO!" at every green light, and "LOOK!" at every animal, bird, or person that you saw. You would call "WATCH OUT!" at every crosswalk or intersection. You laughed loudly when I told you "I might have to gag you or kill you." I am positive that you did not understand all my words but responded to my playful tone. I did, however, love the childish sing-song voice you used when you gleefully announced, "MR. KINGFISHER!" each time we passed the place where a Kingfisher often sat on a wire above the Little River near Trinidad.

It was a relief when you finally stopped wanting to go everywhere with me, preferring to stay in your chair and watch videos. I found myself calling out to Mr. Kingfisher whenever I passed that spot. Now, when I visit the area, I still call to the brave little bird that has surely replaced the original after all this time.

Last Day at Work

We all knew when your last *official* day in the office would be because we helped you retire. Your supervisor and coworkers did a lovely job of coordinating, honoring, celebrating, and documenting your career with captioned photos. I took my own snapshot of you on that last day. You look pleased, leaning back in your chair with your arms crossed, feet propped on your empty desk, and the sun shining on you through the large windows. A few weeks later you got dressed and tried to go back to work. I couldn't find my car keys again and convinced you to change your mind.

A month or so after that, your supervisor, Nancy, called to ask if you would like to come and sit in on a staff meeting. She knew you missed work and thought you might enjoy seeing everyone again and hearing updates on each of the programs you used to oversee. You eagerly accepted her invitation and I promised to drop you off at 8 AM on the date scheduled.

You stayed up late the night before, rifling through papers in your study. I asked what you were doing but didn't press you when you couldn't explain. The next morning you were showered and dressed in your nicest work clothes when I came down to make breakfast. You climbed into the car carrying your briefcase. I asked what was in it and you answered, "That stuff." I felt a murmur of concern but didn't pry. When I picked you up an hour or so later, you were pacing in the lobby and didn't seem ready to leave. You couldn't tell me, but I knew you were upset. Later that day, Nancy called to tell me what had happened.

Rather than quietly sitting and listening, you hijacked the meeting by pulling out your briefcase and showing pictures of yourself as a baby and as an older child. Then you produced diplomas and certificates, pointing to your name each time. You passed around awards and acknowledgements you had received. It was horribly awkward, and no one knew what to do. My heart broke wide open as I listened to her. *You were trying to tell them that you mattered.*

I hadn't noticed that some of the things you had pinned onto bulletin boards and taped to the walls and windows of your study were missing. I finally understood that you were literally trying to hold onto yourself. I began to imagine how terrified you must have been, caught up in a raging stream of dying brain cells that was sweeping you away. This was truly your last day at work.

Last visit to the Study Center

It was a relief when you became more giddy than angry, or frustrated. I could join you in your silliness. We were laughing inappropriately, as usual, when a young neurologist reached across her desk and took both of my hands in her own. Looking directly into my eyes, she said carefully, "This is going to become very, very, difficult." She paused for effect, then added, "He is very strong. You won't be able to do this alone. You MUST prepare and get some legal advice *now,* while he can still participate to some degree." I believed her.

Because of her, I stopped putting off meeting with an attorney who specialized in Elder Law. When I finally did, the attorney explained the legal and financial perils of a diagnosis like this. We managed to transfer titles, deeds, and bank accounts, and to put a Power of Attorney and Advanced Directive in place, so that I could make decisions for you. In just another month or two, you could not have participated. The attorney also provided guidance on how to manage our finances, just in case increasing debilitation led to long-term care in a facility. He stressed that it was important *not to wait for an emergency.* Memory Care facilities cost between $5,000 and $10,000 per month, which quickly consumes most peoples' savings. He provided guidance on how to legally spend resources and keep careful records so there would not be a lapse in your care if our investment savings were depleted before the disease ran its course. The average life expectancy after FTD symptoms begin is 7 years. He educated me about protections for the 'Community Spouse ' that allowed me to retain a percentage of our combined income to live on if our assets were not enough to carry you through to the end. He said that if I had an old car (which I always did), I should consider purchasing a new one because it would likely be the last car I would be able to buy. Our primary home and one vehicle were considered *exempt assets.* When all other assets, including retirement and savings accounts, were depleted, MediCal/Medicaid would subsidize the cost of your care. He assured me that I should be able to stay in our home and retain enough of our income to continue paying the mortgage if this happened. I hoped to keep you with me throughout your illness, but if it proved to be impossible, I believed that I was prepared.

We didn't know it at the time, but the visit to Memory and Aging when the neurologist captured my attention was your last. After more than three years of traveling to San Francisco, you were no longer able to follow directions or respond effectively to questions. It was a relief when the study coordinators decided they would follow up annually through phone calls with me. They remained available as a resource and provided instructions on how to proceed with the autopsy program upon your death. There would be just one more visit, when your brain arrives at the medical center for analysis. It will be your final contribution to the FTD study.

Last Bicycle Ride

You *loved* your bicycle. It was a beautiful cherry red, almost high-end, Trek Road bike. It was light, sleek, and fast. You would wash and caress it like a lover and sometimes I felt jealous. You were a man who would swivel his head to check out every bicycle we passed on the road, much like less disciplined men do with women. As with women, you admired those with a beautiful exterior, but the design and structure underneath is what captured you. You claimed to love your own the most. When you were stressed by work, you would go for a ride. When your doctor said your cholesterol was climbing and wanted you to take statins, you refused, and instead cut back on IPA, ate oatmeal, and rode your bike more. If you needed to think deeply, you went for a longer ride. If you were late coming home from work, I wouldn't check the bars, I'd check the bike shop which is where you spent too much money and time. I once called to ask, "Could you remind Randy that it's his turn to cook dinner tonight?" You came home with pizza and a guilty grin on your face.

You believed that dying of a heart attack or stroke while sitting in a recliner watching TV was a dishonorable death. You proclaimed that you would "Ride until I die!" and planned to be 100 before that happened. You also instructed me that if you crashed and had a Traumatic Brain Injury (TBI), I was "not to allow any dramatic interventions unless there was a good chance of full recovery." You said, "If I can't feed myself, do not feed me." And "If I am lying in my own shit, get a gun." Riding your bike to your final destination was your preferred exit. Allowing you to ride until you ran off a cliff might have extended your quality of life, but it would also have put other people at risk. I had to figure out something else.

For a year or so, friends stepped up and offered to ride with you, even though it still seemed relatively safe for you to occasionally solo ride your routine training routes on roads near our home. The summer before full retirement, you participated in several 100 mile 'century' rides and I noticed that on one of the more mountainous rides, you came in slower than usual and were exhausted. You said that you didn't think you would do that one again. Over the next few months, you got turned around on a routine training ride, taking hours to find your way home. You also had to call me more than once to come and get you, because you no longer knew how to fix a flat tire. Each time you had more difficulty describing where you were so that I could find you. GPS was just becoming available.

These events also frightened you. I think we were both relieved when winter came and you began to ride mostly in the garage on a trainer, unless friends invited you out. The first century ride scheduled for the next spring season was the Farm-to-Forest ride in Willows, CA, where there aren't many hills. You were still a stronger rider than your companions, so we knew you would move out ahead of them. Our friends, Candy and Kent, live in Willows and knew the organizers so were able to alert them to your condition. Everyone agreed to keep an eye out for you and we all cheered you on at the start. After you were out of sight, I decided to drive the route behind you just in case you got separated and took a wrong turn. Sure enough, I hadn't gone far when you passed me, going in the wrong direction, back toward the start line. I turned around, called you back, and got you peddling in the right direction again. By the time you caught up to the pack, you were riding straight into a head wind and began to fall behind. You were struggling. I kept checking in with you, but it seemed that you were in terrible shape. Finally, toward the end of the ride, I convinced you to load your bicycle onto the car and let me drive you the last few miles to the finish. With your earlier detour, you had surely covered the 100 miles anyway. It was after talking with our friend, Eric, who had ridden the first leg with you, that we realized you no longer knew how to shift your gears. He tried to show you, but you were unable to grasp it.

This had probably started a year before on that Century Ride with all the mountains around Crater Lake. Over the winter you mostly trained in the garage where there was no need to shift. During those months you completely forgot how. Willows would be your last bicycle ride.

When we got home, I snuck downstairs and let the air out of your tires. Like the car keys, your pump was "lost" and no matter how hard we both looked, we could not find it. You continued to ride your stationary bicycle to train every couple of days.

I eventually sold your beautiful red road bike to a nice young biologist who was even taller than you. It was a great fit. I had pushed it to the back of the garage for a few weeks so that you would get used to not seeing it. After it was gone, your eyes briefly searched the area where it had been. Unlike the truck, you seemed unsure of what was missing. Once it left your sight, it faded from your memory. Even pictures of you on the bicycle draw no response now. I have stored your engraved dog tags with emergency contacts on one side, and "Ride like the Wind" on the other. Your son, Jordan, will want these one day.

Last time with Financial Responsibility

You enjoyed paying the set monthly bills. There was pride in managing things and you continued to operate the computer for a long while. The last time you made our monthly payments online you forgot to approve the house payment, which I caught just in time to avoid a late payment. When you started ordering things that we didn't need off the internet, and donating to random requests, I quietly blocked your access to our accounts. You could still go online but could no longer access the bank account or credit cards. I also helped to *misplace* your cards. I was getting damn good at pretending to be just as frustrated as you were. I repeatedly feigned helping to look for them until you eventually gave up and began to use your time on the computer looking at pictures and playing music. Oh, and playing solitaire, over and over, for hours and hours.

Last Airplane Ride

Our bucket list included taking another trip to Hawaii before it was too late. It was becoming more stressful to be in unfamiliar places, but you had loved going there so much that I enlisted the help of close friends Dave and Ardeth, and Martha and Eric, who also enjoyed diving and hiking and could help keep you safe. It turned out to be a bittersweet adventure. We had good times with these best friends, took some wonderful hikes and snorkeled, but many things no longer held the significance they once did. And it was not relaxing.

You were a fish biologist who could no longer identify species of fish, or even *say* "fish," although you were still very interested in them. You called them, "those things" while pointing to the water and wiggling your hand.

You became seasick and puked, spewing vomit on the floor and benches in the covered passenger area of the boat that was taking us out to a small island for some snorkeling. I had tried to convince you to move outside where you could see the water, but you refused because it was choppy, and you didn't like the wind. After you vomited, the crew was lightning fast in ushering everyone away. They knew your puking could spread to anyone who heard, saw, or smelled it. Their quick action surely avoided a much larger emergency cleanup. I read somewhere that this contagious gagging and vomiting reflex is thought to be an ancient survival instinct that signaled to a family group that someone had eaten something poisonous. I'm thinking it may have outlived its usefulness.

You didn't seem to recognize ahead of time what that feeling of nausea meant, and then you were confused about how the vomit had come up, using hand signals and expression to describe the surprising experience.

You also did not like getting dirty, so when we took an ATV ride into the mountains, our pictures of you show a dusty, scowling face. You were not having fun. We spent our second week on the Big Island, visiting other friends, Barbara and Ty, who lived up near the volcano. You mostly seemed to enjoy yourself and I considered the trip a success until we arrived at the airport to return home.

A departing plane had been held back for repair; a scheduled arrival was delayed; they were short-staffed. It was hot and the lines were long, winding around the inside and outside of the small airport in Kona. Stress was palpable as people worried about making connecting flights. Babies were crying and everybody was hot and cranky. By the time we got to security, you were the hottest and crankiest. You didn't understand why we had to wait so long and resisted taking off your shoes, emptying your pockets, and removing your watch. I managed to get you to comply with everything except the watch, which you refused to remove before stomping through the metal detector and causing it to flash and buzz. When the agent tried to stop you, you resisted and kept moving forward. I could see other agents running toward us from every corner, one leaping over a barrier, while I tried to explain that you didn't understand. You soon became alarmed also and I shouted *WATCH* holding up my own arm and pointing to my wrist. You frantically pulled it off your wrist but instead of putting it in the container as instructed, you threw it at the agent. The others arrived to tackle you and I tried to block them, waving my arms and shouting, "**Dementia! He doesn't understand!**" By then they knew the watch wasn't an explosive. As they restrained you, they allowed me to explain your illness and agreed to let us go through. Everyone was shaken, including other passengers in line. This was your last airplane ride.

Last trip to Costco

It had been a month or two since you had accompanied me to Costco. Even though there had been incidents of difficult behaviors, it didn't happen every time. You very much enjoyed going and I wanted to keep giving you opportunities to be in your community for as long as possible. On this day, it seemed that circumstances had gathered like ominous clouds to create another perfect storm. Other than the time that you spotted the boy with Down syndrome, my biggest challenge in Costco was usually trying to convince you to select just one movie. Before we walked through the door, I got you to stop and look at me. I spoke slowly, with simple language: "Just ONE (holding a finger up), ONE movie. OK?" "OK!" you said, also holding a finger up. I foolishly relaxed and we walked through the door together.

The first thing you did was head for the DVD display and gather up four or five movies, most that you already had. I tried to get you to put them back but you held them above your head, saying "**No!**" like a child threatening a tantrum. People looked at us strangely and distanced themselves as I pulled my FTD explanation cards out of my bag, and slipped them into my pocket, just in case. I allowed you to put the DVDs in the cart and we started moving through the store to pick up things that we actually needed. I planned to have the cashier remove all but one DVD, when we checked out. You wouldn't know until we unloaded the bag at home.

Next, we encountered a lovely young woman, who lit you up. You smiled brightly as you pointed to her and said loudly to me, "That is a NICE girl." I handed her a card and apologized, as she backed away.

Then you spotted a woman across the aisle with large breasts and proud cleavage. You chortled at the top of your lungs, "ARE THOSE BOOBIES?" She sped off before I could give her a card.

When a pregnant mom with a little girl walked toward us, you were delighted by both. You pointed at her belly, asking with a giggle, "Is *that* girl preggers?" Looking at her daughter, you declared, "That is a *small* girl!" They both looked worried and I reassured them that you were a nice man who loved kids. I gave the mom a card and saw her reading it after we passed.

Not five minutes later, another woman came around the corner on an electric scooter. She rolled into the aisle toward us and your eyes opened wide. You stood stock still and stared as she flew past. She stopped too soon and began to examine the books that were just past us. You quickly moved toward her, closing the distance while pointing and shouting, "WHOA. THAT is a HUGE girl. She is an OLD girl. Is she MESSED UP? Is that a WAGON? That is a HUGE girl. HUGE." The poor woman tried to get away, but you were like a bloodhound on the sent. She weaved and dodged to avoid hitting other shoppers, while I abandoned our cart to run after you both. She was nearly in tears when you finally tired of the chase, and I was able to point you toward a sample table where you could taste food. I apologized profusely and tried to hand her a card, but she threw it down without looking as she rolled off in the other direction. I ran to catch you at the sample table.

Just as I arrived, you pushed your way in front of other people who were already lined up. Before I could stop you, you grabbed several samples and promptly stuffed them into your mouth at once. A moment later, you spit the huge mouthful onto the floor, saying loudly and disgustedly, "That is BAD. What is THAT?"

I placed all my remaining FTD cards on the sample table and encouraged people to take one. As I tried to clean up the mess with napkins, the demonstrator pleaded, "Please don't bother" and watched the crowd move away. You moved too, but toward roasted chickens and the bakery, which you still recognized as tasting just fine. It was time to cut and run.

I grabbed your videos from the cart, holding them up in front of you so you could see them and said, "Let's go!" You followed close on my heels, chasing the videos, as I rushed to check-out. The only thing we bought that day was $60 worth of DVDs that you already had. They didn't ban us from Costco, but I knew for sure you would not be back. That was your last visit.

It took weeks for me to be able to laugh at this episode. One day, as I was telling a friend, she began to chuckle and then, unable to hold back, she erupted into hysterical laughter. She gave me permission to howl at the absurdity of it all and we both laughed until tears ran down our cheeks. I still feel bad for the woman on the scooter and sincerely hope that she continues to go into her community. Life is unpredictable and discomfort is waiting in ordinary moments. Things are not always what they seem but is worth the risk.

Last Birthday Party

In the spring of 2014, I began to plan your 56th birthday party. We had hosted an annual Garden Party each year to celebrate spring and share our slowly developing garden with friends. Our first garden party had taken place 12 years before, when the garden was just a hopeful tangle of weed-covered clay and logging debris. Your birthday in June was the perfect time to share the changes and show off what was blooming. I wasn't sure how long we would be able to continue this tradition, but you still enjoyed having people come to the house and it was difficult for me to let it go. I decided to make it happen.

Over the three years since your diagnosis, we had adjusted to changes as they presented themselves. When it became nearly impossible to take you places, it became just as impossible to leave you home alone. Friends helped from time to time so I could get a break, but this was too much to ask long-term. They had busy lives. I eventually found a man to stay with you when I had to be gone. He was not a caregiver but was kind and not afraid of you, and he could use the telephone to get help. Not long after that, our son Jordan moved home for the summer and was also available to help when he wasn't working. By then, you mostly sat in your chair, but when you didn't, you were increasingly difficult to manage. I was happy to have help for the birthday gathering.

Our favorite local band, Shinbone, agreed to play for a reasonable fee, I bought a truckload of food and beverages and spent days preparing. Friends helped set up while you sat in your chair in front of the TV. You greeted everyone with delighted giggles at seeing them. You were frightened by the fire on your birthday cake but enjoyed the Happy Birthday song. You eventually got out of your chair, and we danced and drank and had a merry time until I realized you had been holding a beer in your hand all evening. After I saw you stagger and then gag, I also realized it wasn't the same one. I got to you in time to guide you into the bathroom to vomit. Five minutes later you were reaching for another beer out of the cooler. I took someone aside and asked him to spread the word that we needed to quickly hide all the alcohol wherever they could find hiding places, while I distracted you. People scattered and the coolers were empty in no time, while the wine bar held only dead soldiers. You kept going from one to the other until you finally gave up. As the crowd thinned out, you settled into your chair to watch one of your movies and began to snooze. Those of us who remained, headed out to the garden where Eric had started a fire in the fire pit. Luckily our friend, Don, from Moonstone Crossing Winery, arrived late with some of his award-winning wine. We were able to make a final toast to you from paper cups, while you were safe in your chair upstairs. I later found wine and beer in the wood pile, tool shed, under garden plants, behind the sofa, and in the dirty laundry hamper. It was a different kind of treasure hunt. This would be the very last garden party.

Last Time Visiting People

During that period, you would still occasionally wander the neighborhood but began to resist going places in the car. Believing that it was important to include you in community activities whenever possible, I would coax you into the car, drive to wherever we were going, coax you out of the car, and then find that you wanted to go home. If we went out to eat, you would always insist on Fish and Chips, even at breakfast. We went to friends for dinner one night and you picked up a full tray of appetizers, sat down on the couch and ate the entire thing. Then, your habit of plugging the toilet with excessive toilet paper, which allowed us to become very close to our plumber, began to happen in restaurants and in other people's bathrooms as well. It was exhausting and entirely too much to impose on others.

One weekend, we had the opportunity to join close friends and their adult children at their beautiful ocean front VRBO vacation house in Mendocino, CA. I was excited to spend time with them and hoped that you would enjoy it as much as you used to when we took diving trips there in years past. We managed to enjoy a few walks on the beach, but you didn't like the wind. You mostly wanted to watch your movies. You were upstairs watching a movie, when someone discovered water dripping from the ceiling in the garage below. You had used the toilet and filled it with paper causing it to overflow. You then sat back down to watch your movie. It was a horrendous mess. You also devoured the children's treats, which had been placed on a high shelf out of sight and out of reach... of children. You guzzled sodas and beer from the coolers and ended the weekend by refusing to relinquish an open beer container as I prepared to drive us home. When I refused to start the car, you weren't concerned and just sat there with your beer. It was a standoff. We sat in the driveway until you finally let someone else retrieve your container through the window. I was pleased when you slept most of the way home. On the drive, I considered that it was no longer fun for you to go to gatherings where you couldn't communicate, and where things were unfamiliar. It wasn't fun for anyone else, either. I gave myself permission to stop making this happen. This was the last time you accompanied me to anyone else's home.

Last Time Alone

When I figured out that you mostly wandered when you couldn't see me for an extended period, I began to run up from the garden to say "Hi" and give you a snack or water every hour or so. Quick trips to the grocery store had to be timed carefully for when someone else was home or while you were watching a movie. If your movie ended while I was still gone, you would look for me and wander into the neighborhood, going into yards and peering through windows if no one answered the door. You had begun to walk down the middle of the street on a blind curve, causing more than one car to swerve into the oncoming lane to avoid you. If you heard a chainsaw, you would hurry over to see what was happening. This once created a terrifying moment for a neighbor who was cutting down a large tree. When I went out for a walk, you might watch me leave and then decide to follow after I had been gone for 15 or 20 minutes. I'd eventually find you walking around looking for me. If anyone stopped to ask what you were doing, you would answer "Hold on." You still looked perfectly normal, and I knew this would not work for any police officer who might be called. I hoped the neighbors would continue to be understanding while I developed strategies.

One day, I helped you to start a movie and ran to the store for just a few things. It was still relatively safe to do this since you almost always watched through to the end. When I returned home 30 minutes later, I found you safely in your chair, still watching your movie. However, you were not alone. A group of strangers was sitting with you. Filling the living room were two sets of adults and three agonized children. When I walked in, everyone but you looked uncomfortable. After seeing the papers on your lap, I recognized them as Jehovah's Witnesses and was able to put together what had happened.

Our house was located down a very long, very private, driveway. Jehovah's mission is to share their version of the gospel, which they felt was important enough to walk onto our property, down the driveway and up two flights of stairs to ring the doorbell. I thank Jehovah we didn't have a vicious guard dog with its own mission.)

By then, you no longer knew what the curious sound of the doorbell meant. However, Gus-Gus certainly did. He was more of a *doorbell dog* than a guard dog. He ran back and forth between you and the door, barking furiously until you finally got up to follow him. When you opened the door, you watched their mouths talk and accepted their pamphlet and likely uttered your alternate standard phrase, "Oh wow." When you turned to go back inside, they followed. When you sat down, they sat down. When they tried to talk to you, you watched your movie. They sat, wondering what to do until I arrived home. I tried not to enjoy their discomfort and worried about the children.

Except for the *Men in Black*, everyone else was silent when I walked in, indicating some comprehension that you didn't understand their words. They had utterly failed in their mission and were clearly relieved to be escorted out. You didn't look up as they moved past your chair. I didn't feel the need to give my usual lecture about religious peddling or respecting our home and personal beliefs. They were uncomfortable enough.

After that, I made sure someone was with you if I left the house. We had just one more scare, when Jordan forgot that you didn't understand words. This was easy to forget because you often nodded as if you did. After I left with a friend to go mushroom gathering in the forest near our home, Jordan told you he was going upstairs to take a shower. When he came back down, your chair was empty, and he could find no sign of you anywhere on the property. We came home a couple of hours later with a bounty of chantarelles and found Jordan frantically searching the neighborhood. I suspected that you had gone into the forest to find us after seeing me with the mushroom gear and watching us walk up the driveway. It was getting dark and we were preparing to call Search and Rescue when we saw you climbing back over the gate from the forest path that we had already searched. You were drenched with sweat and clearly frightened. We were all more careful after that.

Last time Making Love

I have tried very hard to remember the last time we made love. I cannot. It was another gradual letting go. As your illness began to change your personality, medication also tampered with your body chemistry. Authentic affection was less frequent and less appropriate. You became more childlike while I became more maternal. You were still playfully sexual, but it was a behavior rather than a hunger. Nor was it an arousal. While sometimes amusing, it had nothing whatsoever to do with me. Still, I missed the closeness and began to wonder if you did too. I considered that perhaps you just couldn't remember the steps, like when you forgot how to build a fire in the fireplace. One night, after you had snuggled up against me, I kissed you and asked if you wanted to make love. You seemed curious, but unsure what I was asking. I kissed you again and then touched you, thinking that it would give you permission to reach for what you had once so thoroughly

135

enjoyed. Instead of seizing a moment of intimacy, your eyes grew wide, and you began to giggle like a four-year-old who was caught being naughty. I burst out laughing and any thought of romance fled my mind. I have many wonderful memories of lovemaking with you and they are enough. Still, I wish I could remember the last time.

Last Shower

It took me months to realize that the only time you showered was after you rode your training bicycle in the garage. Something about that routine stuck in your mind: Ride, then shower. It made sense when considering you weren't going to work anymore or working in the garden, with each requiring a routine shower before or after. I was relaxed about it for a while because you were still riding in the garage on a regular basis. Every other day, you would fill two water bottles and then put on a bicycle jersey and Lycra shorts. After topping off with a doo-rag, you would trudge downstairs with your shoe clips tapping, to place a Tour de France video into the DVD player across from your trainer. It was good exercise and you enjoyed "Riding with Lance," as you used to say. When I teasingly asked, "Did you beat Lance today?" you would nod and chuckle as if you knew what I was saying. I believe you recognized just one word: Lance.

One day I noticed a bad smell in the garage. I searched around and found that there was fermenting pee in a previously empty garbage can. A lot of it. I showed it to you and asked if you had peed there. You looked worried and said, "No. No pee." You could tell I was not happy, but I wasn't sure if you knew precisely what I was asking. It had clearly been happening for a week or more, but you may not have associated it with the moment when I discovered it. Your instinct was to distance yourself. I said firmly, "PEEING", pointing to your crotch, "happens in the TOILET" pointing upstairs. You looked at me thoughtfully. A few days later, there was pee in the can again, but I discovered it soon after you had put it there. You were sitting in your chair in front of the TV when I confronted you again, saying in a more playful tone, "There is pee in the garbage can AGAIN!" You looked interested and when I grabbed your hand, you followed me. When we got downstairs, I pulled the lid off to show you. This time you smiled brightly and said, "PEE." Unlike before, you seemed very pleased with yourself. You began to explain with your hands and eyes that it was easier to pee in the can than to go upstairs. This is how it was with svFTD. Regardless of how inappropriate something might be, it also made a little bit of sense.

I got you to help me empty and wash the can out, which you did not enjoy. I thought this experience might be a deterrent to future assaults on the garbage can. It wasn't. My next strategy was to try and catch you *before* you relieved yourself. I began to stalk you, sneaking down to the garage and peeking around the door from time to time during your ride. I could also hear your video from upstairs because you played it at top volume. One day when I heard it stop, I raced downstairs to encourage you not to pee in the can at the end of your ride. Rather than follow me upstairs to the toilet, you proudly began to demonstrate how to pee in a garbage can, while cheerfully ignoring my protests. I resigned myself to washing the garbage can on a regular basis. At least you weren't peeing in corners of the house. Yet.

One day, I peeked into the garage and saw you standing next to your trainer, sucking on a water bottle while watching a Tour de France video. You hadn't broken a sweat and it didn't appear that you had been on the bike at all. I kept peeking in like the obsessive voyeur I had become, until the video ended. You never rode. I didn't know if this had happened before, but after Lance once again celebrated his ill-gotten victory, you marched upstairs and changed back into your street clothes without showering. You then placed your cycling clothes in the laundry basket, as if they required cleaning. The ritual of changing into your cycling garb and going downstairs to either ride, or watch Lance ride, continued at less regular intervals for several weeks, eventually stopping altogether. When you stopped climbing onto the trainer, you also stopped showering.

You began to seriously stink. I tried everything to get you into the shower. Food, IPA, boobies, nothing was enticing enough for you to enter the torrent. The more time that passed, the more you resisted. I even got Jordan to try wrestling you in and holding you there, while I washed you. He was very strong, but not strong enough. It wasn't just physical strength that was required of a son to perform that task. We all got drenched and nobody got clean. You occasionally allowed me to wash your hot spots with a washcloth when I caught you in the bathroom, but not often enough. The Living Room began to smell like something had died and I was relieved that the bed upstairs was now mine alone. By then you had days and nights turned around, remaining in your recliner to watch movies when I went upstairs to bed. You eventually refused to lay down at all and began sleeping off and on, day and night, a bit like Gus-Gus. As with other things, I am not exactly sure when the last time you showered was. There would be a steady stream of new 'last times' as your disease continued to progress.

Paddling Against
the Current

I REMAINED HOPEFUL that we could figure out how to keep you at home and out of a facility. Evolving challenges were neutralized as required, with simple deception and straightforward lies. After nearly blowing up the microwave by putting a metal cup in it, I boxed up and stored all metal, leaving only ceramic or plastic. Problem solved for a month or two! Then you put a frozen hamburger in the microwave and timed it for an hour. It caught fire and I unplugged the microwave from behind the cabinet where you couldn't see. I feigned being as mystified by its malfunction as you were. You eventually stopped trying to turn it on. When you tried to stick your hand into a boiling pot of water to retrieve an ear of corn, I was more diligent about keeping lids on and never again left a pot unattended. When you began consuming entire loaves of bread, jars of nuts, bags of chips, or cookies, these foods were stored with the alcohol and soda in a locked wine closet located downstairs near the garage.

Sometimes the yin-yang of it all was amusing. After you developed a fear of fire, it was easy to keep you away from the gas stove, but you kept blowing my decorative candles out, often from an impressive distance. When you became afraid of the dark, you stopped going outside at night, which was a relief, but then you turned on every light in the house. If I came down to check on you in the middle of the night, it was not unusual to find the dining table carefully set and you sitting patiently in your chair at one end. You'd ask, "Is that coming in here now?" and pat your coffee cup or plate. It might be 2 AM but you were hoping for breakfast. Exhaustion was creeping in.

After you got lost in the woods, you became less enticed by things outside of your immediate environment and stopped wandering the neighborhood. Eventually you also stopped getting out of your chair, except to eat meals or use the bathroom. I was saddened but secretly pleased, because it renewed my hope that you could remain with me in our home. I no longer had to worry about you getting hit, lost, shot, crushed, or arrested. Things felt more manageable for a few months more.

You were not incontinent. You knew when you had to go and could hold it. However, the deliberately inappropriate peeing that started in the garbage can, now happened on the front and back porch. No one could physically stop you from pissing when and wherever you wanted. You still mostly used the toilet but would sometimes randomly jump up, open the front door, and urinate on the door jamb. One day UPS was delivering a package just as you walked outside. You smiled and very carefully drenched the box that he had just set down. The guy jumped back and ran for his truck, roaring up the driveway in a cloud of dust. Perhaps he thought it was a political statement about Amazon. Occasionally, you seemed to want to also drop your pants but hesitated, perhaps because the chair on the porch had a pillow on it which did not resemble a toilet. You continued to use the toilet for approximately another year. I didn't know at the time, but these little tendencies forewarned of a new set of challenges that would require even more creative remedies. Inappropriate pooping and pissing are some of the things many people have difficulty talking about. This is different than *incontinence*, which is usually about lack of control, but many use that term anyway.

As your vocabulary became increasingly limited, a few jingles, song lyrics, and sayings like "I'm your Huckleberry!" from the movie *Tombstone*, remained accessible for a long while. For months you could channel *Forest Gump:* "I may not be a smart man, but I know what love is" while smiling tenderly at me, until that link was also severed. Eventually, responses to all questions became,

"Oh Wow!" or "Hold on!" You learned that if you used either of these phrases, people almost always laughed, which pleased you too.

Despite your good nature, your behaviors and physical needs gradually became more difficult, more expensive, and more unsafe for us all. I still couldn't get you into the shower, and then you began to absolutely refuse to get into the car for a doctor or dentist appointment, or anything else. I also couldn't stop you from swallowing whatever looked interesting and began hiding or locking up medicines and certain chemicals. The last time you were at the dentist, the hygienist asked you to gargle with mouthwash from a little paper cup which you tossed down your throat and swallowed like a shot of tequila. Her eyes searched mine in alarm, "Oh my!"

I began to understand what the neurologist had been talking about when she warned that I would not be able to do this alone. I could see more clearly what was coming and knew I couldn't protect you if you stopped responding to my coercion and manipulations. I couldn't keep you clean and knew this would worsen as you required more physical care. I was also having trouble maintaining the house and property while caring for you. I needed additional help which depleted our savings even more quickly. Friends couldn't keep filling the gaps and I couldn't watch you every second. I also couldn't physically stop you. The next phase of FTD was blowing its hot breath in our direction and I knew it would be foolish to just sit back and wait for the emergency that was surely headed our way.

I started to research and evaluate care options in our area for a 6'3", 180 pound, 55-year-old man who was physically strong and did not respond to verbal requests or cues. There were *none*. Not one. No facility in our area would accept you. Furthermore, no caregivers trained in dementia care were willing to come into our home because of the same concerns about your size and the difficulty this would present as your disease progressed.

The Elder Law attorney had carefully set things up so that

if you required a facility, I would not lose our home after other resources were spent down. That was only helpful if you were close by. We had no idea that there was not a care facility near our community that would accept you. Also, if any one of them agreed to, they would evict you when our money ran out because they refused to accept the MediCal/Medicaid supplement amount if we could no longer pay the full monthly charges. I knew you could live well beyond the average life expectancy of seven years. I also knew that our savings would not last more than a few more years.

The attorney had neglected to inform us that care facilities are not required to accept MediCal/Medicaid insurance. They often deliberately neglect to certify with these funding sources so they can more easily refuse low-income applicants. The two that did accept MediCal were full and refused to put you on their wait list for the reasons we already knew. They were also afraid of you.

The warning to not wait for an emergency took on a new urgency. An acceleration of dangerous behaviors could land you in jail, a psychiatric hospital, or an emergency placement which would force us to accept any facility that would agree to take you, even if it was located hundreds of miles away. There would be no longer be a choice. The search for an appropriate placement jumped to the top of my priority list.

Surrender

Finding the peace in surrender

Over the Waterfall

SOUTHERN OREGON IS where my family lived and where I decided to start my search. It was just a three-hour drive and I thought that if we could get you safely settled there, I might be able to split my time between both communities. I still hoped to keep our home.

My daughter, Kari, worked at an assisted living facility that was part of an aging-in-place complex, so I made an appointment there. They offered independent living for those not yet requiring any assistance, but also offered assisted apartments and cottages when assistance became necessary, including early and manageable stages of dementia. Most important to us was the separate locked memory care facility for those who developed advanced dementia. The buildings were in a neighborhood setting with lawns and pathways for safe strolling. The complex was also located just two miles from the assisted living facility where my mother was living, which would be convenient.

I met with managers of both the memory care and assisted living facilities. After an evaluation, they felt that you weren't quite ready for memory care and recommended assisted living until you were. You were no longer wandering and could still feed, dress, and toilet yourself. You needed supervision, laundry, meals, and hygiene assistance, but spent your days and nights alternating between sleeping, watching movies, or playing solitaire on the iPad. If something came up, there was a team of people to help you and keep you safe. There were also several other residents in the assisted living facility who were also in an early stage of dementia. Most importantly, they promised a "seamless transition" into their locked memory care building when it was needed. No worries about acceptance! I was thrilled to think of you in this less restrictive environment without risking future chaos if an emergency placement became necessary. They also reassured me that if you were established in their care before we ran out of money, they would accept Medicaid. I applied.

Less than a month later, the manager of Assisted Living left a message saying that she had a studio apartment available for you. I didn't call back for three days. It felt like I had been paddling against the current for a very long time, but now I was above a waterfall. If I stopped paddling, we would be swept over and there would be no going back. On my second night of agonizing, you emptied an entire cupboard of food onto the floor while searching for cookies and chips. You then pulled a dozen packages out of the freezer. I found them on the island, thawed and waiting for me in the morning. After that, you stuffed an entire roll of toilet paper in the upstairs toilet again and flooded two floors. The plumbing bill was cheaper than the ceiling repairs, not to mention the cleaning.

I hadn't had a full night's sleep for many weeks when I made the call. They assured me that they dealt with toilet clogs all the time. The lights were always on and the kitchen was locked, but someone was always available to help you with food if you came searching during the night. I recognized it as an opportunity that may not come again.

Four years after your diagnosis, I wrote a check and signed the papers for you to enter a long-term care facility. You would not be coming back home.

The next few weeks were a blur as I drove back and forth, making arrangements. You needed medical clearance, and I needed to meet with Oregon Senior and Disability Services so that I was sure of their requirements. Savings were nearly depleted and retirement accounts shrinking. You needed a bed, dresser, table, etc. I needed to prepare to be away from home for an extended period so I could help you settle in.

After struggling mightily to get you into the car so the doctor could provide your medical clearance and vaccinations, I realized that Jordan and I would need more help for the big move. I called

our close friends, Ardeth and Dave, who had introduced us 18 years before. They lived in Washington but were retired and had the time and energy to do this. They also loved you. When I asked them to come, there was no hesitation. I could count on them.

At some point, it occurred to me that I would also need to find a place to stay in Oregon because my family could not accommodate me. The facility said I could stay with you for the first week or so, but after you adjusted I would need to sleep and eat elsewhere, or be charged. After looking at rental prices, I decided that a small RV might work, and contacted the facility manager to ask if I could park one in their outer lot so I would be close by. Once you were comfortable, I planned to park it for just a few days each week. They gave me their blessing, and the very next day I opened a search page and found a sweet little Rialta Winnebago for sale. I bought it with some help from my mother and set it up for Gus and me. It was much cheaper than renting and we could be close to you and comfortable at the same time.

Moving Day

Your last day in our home was bittersweet. Bitter because you didn't know you were leaving home and never coming back. Sweet because I found a place for you where I would no longer have to worry about keeping you safe as your illness progressed and our funds were depleted. And they promised to get you into the shower!

Ardeth and Dave arrived from Washington the day before, and Jordan arranged to take time off work so he could see you off and help get you into the car. We would drive two cars and caravan the 150 miles along beautiful ocean beaches and cliffs, past lagoons and through forested river canyons. Once you were settled, Ardeth and Dave would head back to Washington, and I would stay with you until you forgot that you didn't want to be there. I would then drive back to fetch the RV camper and

Gus-Gus, who was in Mexico with our dear friends, Margie and Tom.

That morning we had breakfast and then began walking past you in your chair. You watched as we went back and forth, in and out, and up and down the porch stairs, carrying things out of the house and putting them in cars. I had already furnished your new room, but you needed towels and linens, along with your clothing and other personal items. You sat in your recliner, as usual, holding your iPad and playing solitaire while watching a movie. I remember you curiously looking up from time to time, and even walking to the window to look down and watch us loading the cars before sitting back in your chair. I kept saying excitedly, "We're going on a trip!" When we were finally ready, I gathered up all your movies and said, "C'mon, let's go!" You saw the movies and got up to take them back. I was ready for this and sprang into action, running out the door and down to the car, holding them above my head and calling "C'mon, Randy Man. We're going on a trip!" You followed me out to the porch but stopped at the landing, somberly studying us as we stood together in the driveway. Beckoning. After a few minutes you turned around and walked back inside, then closed and locked the door. I had a key.

I made you a mocha and tried to entice you into the car with it. You walked all the way down the stairs, but then refused to reach into the car to retrieve it and returned to the house. I made you a berry smoothie, which you loved even more than mochas, and I even sang, "It's Smoothie Smoothie Time", while dancing and waving it around in the air to entice you back outside and down the stairs. This time Jordan was ready to lock the door behind you, which he did the minute you stepped out. He ran to lock the other doors from the inside when you appeared to be headed in their direction. We enticed you back down to the car and I held the smoothie so you could see it waiting for you. This time you took it but refused to get into the car. You were holding your iPad in your other hand and Dave, who was casually standing next to the car, reached his hand out and asked to see it. Surprisingly, you handed it to him. He placed it in the car on the seat next to where we wanted you to sit and stepped aside as you reached in for it. Then he firmly blocked you from behind, holding tightly to the car frame when you tried to back out. You shuffled and shoved but finally gave in, resignedly muttering, "Oh Wow" and sitting down. You put your seat buckle on like you'd been doing it every day and began sipping on your smoothie while playing solitaire on the iPad. When we leapt into our cars and sped up the steep driveway, you calmly looked up from the back seat and began to watch out the front windshield. Luckily it was a sunny day so we could crack the windows to let your stink out. *Phew!* You settled down and curiously watched the scenery speed by as we drove North on Hwy 101, a road you had ridden on your bicycle hundreds of times. When we drove over Little River, you did not call out to "Mr. Kingfisher," nor did you even once turn around to look out the back window. You continued leaning forward, looking toward whatever the future would bring.

Ardeth and Dave got to the facility first to set up your TV and DVDs, along with your obnoxious singing stuffed animals, sheets and familiar bedspread, and your favorite throw for the new recliner. They put pictures on your wall that you would recognize. I knew when we drove up to the building that it would look like a hotel to you and hoped that would entice you to go inside. It did. We walked around the lobby for a bit and then I showed you the key to your room. You walked down the hall with me to find it. We opened the door to see Ardeth and Dave waiting to greet you. "Surprise!" They invited you to sit in your new recliner and handed you the remote. You started a movie but kept looking out the window at our car in the parking lot. You were confused. After a while you got up and took my hand to lead me out the door. I walked with you down the hall until we came to the big front doors and then I turned back, saying, "We're staying here for a while," and led you back. That evening, when we sat down to dinner in the big dining room with the other residents, it felt like a restaurant. They didn't have Fish and Chips, but you ate well. Then you got up to leave, again pulling me toward the door. Ardeth and Dave helped by distracting you and giving high-fives while I convinced you to sit back down. You liked high-fiving and would chuckle, "five, ten," and continue counting up by fives as long as they would participate. We once got you up to 100. After dinner, Ardeth and Dave were exhausted and left for their hotel. You and I went back to your room and watched your movies until we both got sleepy. I tried to get you to lay down on the bed, but you refused, staying in the recliner just like you did at home. I was pretty confident that you wouldn't leave while I was there with you, but I didn't sleep well and kept checking all night. You were still there the next morning when a caregiver popped her head in to say, "Good morning," and invited us to breakfast.

Ardeth and Dave also came for breakfast and you seemed happy to see them. Even so, you would periodically stand up and pull on my hand, trying to get me to leave. Eventually you left the table by yourself and walked through the big glass front doors and out into the icy cold morning. You didn't have a coat on. Several people started to chase you and I stopped them, wanting to give you the opportunity to come back inside on your own. I knew that you were looking for the car. When you spotted it you walked over and tried to open the door. You went from one door to the other, moving all the way around the car several times, and then you just stood there, looking back at me through the glass doors. You were starting to shiver when I walked outside, calling to you, "Hey, Randy Man, it's COLD out here," wrapping my arms and shivering exaggeratedly. "C'mon back inside!" beckoning with my hand before turning back in. You pulled on a car door again and looked toward me, again. We all watched you stand there for a minute longer, and then you slowly began walking back toward the building. You opened the big front door and came back inside on your own. We greeted you with big smiles and a cup of coffee.

It took just three days for you to be oriented and comfortable there. You especially enjoyed being able to go out and get coffee whenever you wanted. That was to become a problem, but initially it was a bonus. I began leaving you for a 30-minute walk and you stayed put. I then began leaving to have an hour-long meal elsewhere and you still stayed put. I began visiting my mother for a couple of hours at a time and you were just fine. Two weeks later, we got you into the shower.

The two male care givers and I were just as wet as you were. One of them couldn't stick it out and escaped before the mission was completed. He stayed long enough to help pull the door closed when you repeatedly tried to open it, but then went Missing in Action. The other worked with me all the way through, enticing, pushing, blocking, and pulling the door back each time you managed to get it partially open. We were in there for well over an hour. When we finished, the shower curtain was hanging off the rod, water covered the floor, and we were all red faced and exhausted. Margie was back from Mexico and had been sitting in the hallway safely out of harm's way and listening. Her comment afterwards was, "Well, that was one wild rodeo." Everybody in the building could hear the ruckus, but you smelled great again and there was ice cream waiting for you. Margie and I went for a drink.

After that, two people came twice a week for your shower. While you didn't willingly go in, you never again fought so hard. You knew that there would be a reward when you came out. I stayed with you for three weeks before it felt safe to leave you overnight. You refused to go outside, day or night, even when I tried to get you to walk with me. We didn't have to worry about you leaving and getting into trouble. At least not yet. I drove back to our home to retrieve the RV and the dog.

Living in the Parking Lot

I parked the van in the far back corner of the facility compound near the memory care building where we believed you would one day be living. The place where we parked was an unpaved area that was fairly private. Gus and I developed a schedule of waking up and checking in on you to say "Good Morning" before going for a walk. We walked about a half mile to a neighborhood store where they had great coffee. I would buy a large coffee with extra cream to go, and we would walk through the garden of a nursery nearby while I sipped it. After that we would head back to your room and hang out for an hour or so, then leave again, coming and going off and on each day. You got used to me being gone and became comfortable with the staff, seeming to enjoy them coming in and out as well.

As people got to know us, you began looking forward to going to the dining room and slapping a high five on anyone who would allow it. It was your greeting. Some people were kind and would engage, laughing with you. Others were uncomfortable and would refuse, looking away. A few were rude and nasty (one called you a "retard" and another ordered you to "get away" giving you a push). I'm guessing they had another form of brain disfunction.

Most people were curious about you. They wanted to know how old you were and what had happened to you. None had heard of FTD. I spent lots of time telling them who you were, what had happened, and why we chose Assisted Living as the first stop to dementia care. I gave as much information about your disease as they wanted, but they were mostly interested in the personal stories. It is when I shared those that you became a person, rather than an annoying curiosity.

One very nice elderly man, who used a walker, seemed especially sympathetic at first, and kept imploring me to come and pray with him. He was a Christian minister and convinced that God would cure you if we just asked fervently enough. He insisted that he had made it happen before and he wanted it to happen now. It soon became clear that he *really* wanted it to happen now. Eventually, he began to complain to management that you didn't belong there. I had a conversation with him about you not yet being ready for Memory Care and he asked me why I couldn't "just take you home or put you somewhere else." You weren't even a problem yet but clearly made him uncomfortable on several levels.

There was a younger woman with no legs who was in a motorized wheelchair. She was very friendly and thought you were "extremely handsome" and often stopped by your room for a visit. One day she asked me if we still had sex. I told her that was a "very personal question." A few minutes later, she asked whether you could still "get it up." I thought for a moment, then responded, "No. But if you could, you wouldn't fool around because that would hurt my feelings." I later learned that she had a history of inviting men to come and have a little fun with her. I don't think it would have worked out for the two of you.

I planned to drive back and forth between home and Oregon every three days. Instead, something would often come up to keep me from leaving, or I would need to turn around and drive right back after just a day at home. Then the facility had a management change, and the new director did not like my van parked in the back lot because it set precedent for others to do the same. She asked me to find another place close by, but there were none. She extended her permission if I promised to keep looking. During those weeks, as I drove back and forth, I was reminded how treacherous Pacific Northwest highways could be. In the summer there are lines of slow-moving RVs with impatient locals trying to pass them. In the winter there are rockslides, ice, snow, and raging winds that topple trees. They are listed among the most dangerous roads in the country. I began to realize that I couldn't do that drive for the multiple years it would likely require and started thinking about selling our home and moving close to you. I wasn't sure how I would do it, but knew I needed to.

Soon after, Gus and I were walking in the quiet little neighborhood of homes directly behind the facility buildings, when we struck up a conversation with one of the residents. Dan also had a Yorkshire terrier named Bailey. I asked if houses ever came up for sale there and he said he thought the house across the street was going on the market. I contacted the owner who said he couldn't wait for me to sell my house, which I hadn't even listed yet, but offered to stay in touch. We exchanged phone numbers.

Two days later, I drove back to our home, walked slowly up the stairs to the front porch, through the front door and then through every room of our house. I went into your office with all your awards and photos, then into the living room where your big TV was still waiting. I wandered into the kitchen where everyone seemed to end up during gatherings. I went out the back door and onto the deck, looked out at the gardens, the pond, and the forest beyond. I ran my hand across the railing and let my feet move down the stairs and then walked every path and crossed the little bridge you had built. I touched the stones you had placed and brushed my hand across the grasses, trees and shrubs I had planted. I sat down on our bench above the pond and after a few minutes, stood up again and screamed. I wailed like a creature from the swamp and sobbed until I was empty. I didn't care if anyone heard me. When I finally quieted, I noticed that the neighborhood and the surrounding forest was utterly silent. Nothing moved.

I recalled a similarly desperate scream years before. It emitted from shrubbery planted next to the driveway of my house in Redding. I frantically searched and found a tiny black and white kitten with eyes barely open, who had been left behind in the cold. How he was able to emit such a fierce sound is still hard to comprehend. I picked him up, fed him, kept him warm and loved him with everything I had. I realized I needed to do that for myself. My life was once again being irrevocably altered.

When I woke up the next morning, I called a trusted realtor, Sally, and made an appointment for her to list our house. It sold before a sign went up. On the day we opened escrow, I received a call from the owner of the house behind the memory care facility in Oregon. The contract with his realtor had ended and his property hadn't sold. He wondered where I was with my property and I informed him that mine had. We immediately struck a deal.

Escrows closed simultaneously and I moved to Southern Oregon on June 15th, 2015. I left our home, our gardens, and our dear friends, to live where I could see you every day and make sure that you were well cared for. Things fell into place like a puzzle with matching pieces and a new chapter opened for both of us.

The Great Escape

You had been in assisted living for nearly four months when you began peeing on the window. It didn't happen every day but required clean up a couple of times a week. Staff began coming to toilet you every couple of hours, which seemed to stop it. It also provided additional attention, which you enjoyed. You were content and settled down again. Other than rare walks with me around the compound, neither you, nor your singing stuffed gorilla companion, left the building without me. The gorilla, which sang "Wild Thing," was about 18 inches tall. I had it delivered to your office as a surprise Valentine's Day gift seven years before. Initially an amusement, it became your amassador after you lost the ability to communicate. You would hold it up to visitors and push its button to audibly greet them while also laughing maniacally. You brought it with you to assisted living and kept it next to your chair.

I felt safe planning a much needed get-away to join old childhood friends for a weekend of good food, conversation, and no responsibilities. I loaded up my little RV and pulled into the parking lot in front of your facility to check in with staff before saying goodbye to you and hitting the road. I later realized that I was in full view of your only window, which looked directly onto that parking spot after Gus-Gus and I waved goodbye and walked outside to climb into the van, excited to be off for an adventure.

I was driving through the agricultural checkpoint on the California border, when I received a frantic phone call. They had been trying for an hour to get through. Soon after we left, you had walked out of your room carrying several DVD's and your gorilla. They tried to engage you, but you moved straight past the reception desk, headed out the front doors and into the parking lot. The DVDs and the gorilla were your two most precious possessions.

After walking around the parking lot for a while, you began walking the paths between the buildings. Staff valiantly took turns walking with you and trying to redirect you back, but you refused, walking faster and more determinedly away from them and their protection. When you did not tire, they began calling me to return. The calls went to voice mail because I was in the mountains. They were preparing to call the police when I answered. You had begun moving toward the highway.

I told them I would get there as soon as possible and begged them to do whatever they could to contain you before calling the police. I turned the van around and focused on not getting a speeding ticket. Nearly three hours had passed by the time I pulled back into the facility parking lot. Staff greeted me with exhausted relief and reported that when you started toward the highway again, they had surrounded you, offered food, and enticed you into the memory care building, which has locks on the doors. You had been pacing that facility and repeatedly trying the doors for over an hour before I arrived.

The Manager's office in memory care has a large observation window looking into the common area. I stood with her as she pointed to you through the window, where we could watch you frantically pace around and around the large room, trying doors over and over as you went, and still clutching tightly to your gorilla and DVDs. She commented that you, "Seemed very confused, like you were looking for something." I responded, "He's looking for me." She didn't think so. She believed you were experiencing hallucinations or a break from reality, which was frightening you. I said, "Watch this," and walked through the door that opened into the common area. As soon as you saw me, you rushed over and took my hand to lead me out. When they buzzed us out the front door, you pulled me across the grounds toward your Assisted Living building. You walked me inside, down the hall, and into your room. You shut the door and would not let go of my hand until I sat down. You were sweaty and exhausted. I got someone else to walk the dog for me and sat with you as we ate a late dinner and watched one of your videos together. You stood up and for the first time in weeks, you peed on the window. It seemed that you thought you were peeing outside.

By the time we cleaned it up, it was after 10 pm. I crawled into your bed, and you crawled in with me. You had not laid in a bed for nearly a year, but you wrapped yourself around me from behind, like in the old days, and slept all night without moving. I was afraid to move. I lay very still as I listened to you breathe. We never slept together again.

After your Great Escape, something changed in your brain. You remembered you liked being outside and that it felt good to move your body. You began walking on the paths several times a day but didn't wait for someone to walk with you. You didn't try to go to the highway and always came back to your room after loping around the buildings, but we knew this could change without notice. Nobody was comfortable with you walking alone. Soon after, you stopped sitting in your seat in the dining room and began following the serving cart around and taking what you wanted from it. You also began filling your coffee cup every hour, which made you walk even faster and pee more often. You began pissing on the windows in the common area, and then moved to the tables in the dining room. I once caught you standing in front of a table that had just been set with fresh linens and dishes. I grabbed an empty glass just in time, which you were delighted to fill with perfect aim. No one, including myself, could stop you without tremendous effort. You didn't hit or shove, you just persisted. I did a lot of explaining and apologizing as I tried to mitigate your impact. It was time for memory care.

I met with the Director of assisted living, who had already met with their staff nurse. They agreed that you needed to move as soon as possible, except their memory care didn't have an empty bed. While we waited for an opening, your behaviors worsened. They required me to stay with you around the clock because they didn't have enough staff to follow you around. While they were obligated by law to increase your level of care as your needs increased, your needs were unique. It was too much to ask of anyone. They also had other people to care for. I was exhausted and friends traveled long distances to give me occasional breaks so I could sleep.

Your fear of the dark also dissipated and you began to walk into the neighborhood behind the compound every few hours throughout the night. One night, at around 2 AM, I woke up to the sound of the door closing. I rushed out after you in my bare feet. You moved at such a fast pace and with your long legs I had difficulty catching up. I tried to get you to hold my hand, which would sometimes slow you down, but you refused. The residents of a large house that sat directly behind the compound had left their garage door open and the light was on. It lit up the darkness and drew you in like a moth to flame. In this rural community, many people have guns. It was not hard to imagine someone defending their property or themselves from a 6'3" middle-of-the-night intruder who refused to respond to questions or leave when commanded. I became more terrified when I considered the homeowners may have also forgotten to lock the interior door from the garage into their house. A rush of panic filled me with adrenaline as you headed into the garage. It gave me the strength to run ahead of you and physically block you while shouting, "NO!" and pushing you back at the same time. We were both surprised at my strength as I backed you up and then firmly grabbed your hand. After several attempts to get around me, you let me lead you away. Memory care was now an urgent need.

The next day I checked with the manager who still didn't have a bed but promised to help find you one nearby. They needed you out of there. I reminded them that I bought a house in the neighborhood so I could be close to you. I knew that if I moved you outside of their community, they would not be obligated to take you back. It would negate their promise of the 'seamless transition' that was already compromised. The manager of memory care personally promised me that she would "absolutely take you back" stressing that we needed to focus on safety now. She stated that the "very first opening in the men's wing" would be yours. She *promised*.

You were accepted into a smaller, well designed memory care facility across town. I called good friends, Candy and Kenton, and my daughter Kari, to help move you again. It required more planning, creative strategizing and manipulation, along with a rented truck. We arranged for Kari to take you on a long ride around town after enticing you into her car with food, as usual. As soon as she set out, we dismantled your room and threw everything into the truck, then drove to your new facility where we frantically unloaded and put things back together. It took nearly two hours. During this time Kari took you to a drive-up fast-food place and got you a hamburger with fries to eat in the car. She soon called to say you had eaten everything. I told her to drive around some more and then go get more French fries. She called again and I told her to keep driving around, and then go get ice cream. Each time she called; we would work faster. I don't remember how many miles she drove, or how much food you ate, but she was a true hero that day! By the time you were trying to escape the car at traffic lights, we were ready. All your belongings, your bed, recliner, your TV with DVDs, your gorilla, and pictures were in place. We were waiting to greet you when she drove up. We helped you out of the car and took you inside. When we walked into your room, you were understandably confused again, seeing all your things in another new environment.

We showed you the bathroom, which you immediately used. Then we started a movie and sat with you for a while. When the others left, you also tried to leave. The door was locked. You kept trying but it didn't budge. I stayed with you for three nights (the magic number), until you stopped trying to leave. They had a nice outdoor patio that you could access any time you wished. There was also an open common area with the kitchen in the middle. It was homier than the larger facility, and I thought it would be a good transition for you. On the fourth day I went home and slept for twelve hours.

The Less Great Escape

On your fifth day in the new locked facility, I received another frantic phone call telling me that you had left the building. You were again refusing to be redirected back and were walking toward a very busy street just a block away. They were also preparing to call the police. I dropped what I was doing and drove over to find that they had managed to get you back inside. It had taken several staff members to corral you. I asked what had happened and one of the staff said she thought a visitor had held the door open for you.

The next morning, I was called to a meeting with the Staff Nurse, the Manager, the Assistant Manager, and the Director. The nurse was very much in charge. I expected groveling apologies. Instead, he began by stating that they did not think they would be able to "*meet your needs.*" This is language you do not want to hear. When I asked him to clarify, he said very stridently, that "HE put everyone here in danger!" I was stunned. Looking around the room, others seemed to be following his lead. I pointedly asked, "How did Randy get out of the door?" He hesitated and then confirmed that "another family member didn't think he looked like a resident and opened it." I paused for a moment, waiting for someone else to catch this, but there was silence. I responded, "It sounds like THAT PERSON put everyone in danger, especially Randy!" He seemed unable to absorb what I said and continued about how many staff members had to chase you, and how you refused to follow directions, and that they were forced to leave other residents alone and unattended. I took a deep breath and slowly reminded him that this was precisely why you had been placed in a locked facility with trained staff. I heard my own voice rise as I suggested that they had a policy issue and might want to consider not providing the door code to anyone who didn't agree not to open it for someone else. The meeting ended when I stood up and suggested that you had helped them identify a potential liability. I expressed confidence that we could work together to meet your needs along with everyone else's. And then I left.

A week later, the same determined nurse wanted to remove you again because you kept high-fiving everyone, including little old ladies with walkers. If they didn't participate by raising a hand, you would pat their heads and count, five, ten, fifteen... until someone distracted you. You once high-fived the nurse, who slapped your hand away and shouted, "NO, RANDY!" He then accused *you* of being dangerous. He called another meeting and I explained that most behaviors are an unmet need. Your need at that moment was to connect. I suggested that we encourage staff to *smile* and grab your hand each time you tried to high-five anyone, and then hold it warmly for just a few counts before letting go. They would then walk away with a smile and say, "Later Gator." Three days (someone should do a study on the three-day thing) after implementing this strategy, you stopped high-fiving and held hands, like a long handshake, for just a moment. Your need was met, and everyone seemed happy. With one notable exception.

As new behaviors surfaced, we collaboratively came up with creative ways to modify and mitigate them. It was tedious, but nearly everyone began to relax and enjoy you. You were gentle and sweet, as well as playful and silly. After a while, they forgot about your size.

In the meantime, I kept checking with the memory care facility closer to me. The Manager repeatedly said that they still had no openings. One evening, I was walking Gus-Gus past their front door and noticed a woman helping to move an elderly man into the facility. She told me that they had called her a few nights before, saying there were two beds available. The next morning, I walked into the Manager's office and reminded her of her promise. She was embarrassed and upset, saying she had "no choice." While she was unable to confirm that they had overruled her, it seemed that the corporate management had never planned to accept you back once you were moved. Like the other facilities we investigated, they did not want a 6'3", 56-year-old man with dementia behaviors in their dementia facility. This manager would eventually leave that position because of their lack of integrity. She became a staunch advocate and creative problem solver, training managers and care staff of other facilities around the area how to provide true person-centered care. It turned out to be a win for others in the community.

I surrendered to the realization that, despite the nurse, the place you were in was better for you. You had a private room with a bathroom and had already adjusted. While I had hoped you would be housed conveniently across the street from me, it was only a few miles away and I probably would have bought the house I lived in anyway. I also liked the manager at your new facility. She was still learning, but a wonderful person who tried very hard to do a good job and had a great sense of humor. She saw each resident as an individual and developed a special bond with you. We all settled down, except for the dominating nurse. The manager seemed to have difficulty managing his behaviors.

Offerings

IT IS VALENTINE'S Day and I have selected the perfect gift for you. A Google search provides several origin stories about this unofficial holiday, but I find just one to be believable: Saint Valentine was beheaded on February 14th, 269 AD, because he had defied Roman Emperor II, Claudius the Cruel, by uniting couples in marriage after it was forbidden. Claudius was reported to be a pagan who believed that wives prevented men from joining his army.

If this is true, then St. Valentine was surely inspired by his Roman Catholic faith. We know the church does not ring bells for *unholy* matrimony. I imagine that Valentine may not have fully considered that his quiet rebellion might also encourage couples to express love and commitment in ways of their own choosing, ways he hadn't intended. Faith and courage are not the same, yet each may set us on a righteous, and treacherous, path.

This is the 20th Valentine's Day since you and I became a couple. It is the first that we will celebrate in a locked memory care facility. Your dementia has misplaced or erased what you once knew about the delights of romance and reciprocal giving.

Today I re-gift a piece of jewelry to myself, from you. You will receive a fresh chocolate heart in exchange. I examine my delicate silver pendant, turning it around slowly, just as I did ten years ago when you first gave it to me. One side is beautifully etched with tiny flowers and grasses, while the other is engraved with words: *Out beyond, there is a field. I will meet you there.* While not a direct quote, this reminds me of the 13th century mystic, Rumi.

You wanted it to remind me of our love for uncivilized spaces like the wildlife garden we created together. Our garden invited the winged, hoofed, pawed, toothed, and clawed to visit. It enticed crawlers, tunnelers, hoppers, swimmers, nesters, browsers, and pollinators to share that small piece of earth with us. Once we surrendered to them, we discovered a refuge for ourselves. The stresses of our busy lives fell away as we planted, cleared paths, placed stones, and then sat quietly to watch. You told me you discovered this pendant while searching for something that referred to a garden. "Field" was a compromise, but you were confident that these words would carry the message. They still do.

When I arrive in your room, I hold my necklace up and say, "Thank you for this." You glance at it without recognition and turn your attention to the chocolate heart, which you accept with a chuckle. Once the chocolate has disappeared into your mouth, you abruptly stand and head to the common area to see what all the noise is about.

Family members have been invited to attend a surprise musical performance for Valentine's Day. We watch as a 20+ year-old Michael Jackson impersonator grabs his crotch and moonwalks to the sound of "Billy Jean." The performer is the son of one of the care staff who offered him up for free, which is an attractive price.

As unlikely as it might seem, I observe two of the more elderly gentlemen smiling and nodding their heads to the music. I have never seen the full face of one man, who lifts his grizzled head from its usual position of chin-on-chest to watch with faded grey eyes and a huge, unrestrained, grin of delight.

Michael Jackson does not hold your attention. Beautifully decorated heart-shaped cookies do. They have been placed on a card table in the middle of the kitchen with the hope that they will be out of your long-armed reach. It is my job to distract you from the cookies today and I fail miserably. After months of living here, this is the day you discover how easily your long legs can climb over the gate and into the kitchen.

We are soon back in your room, happily munching pink-frosted cookies, which were shamelessly used to inspire you to follow me. I hold my cookie up in victory, touching yours for a toast. With gusto, I say, "To Howard!" which has been our annual Valentine's Day salute for years. Cookies do not clink like wine glasses, but it is still a satisfying gesture. I know that it is the cookie and not the memory of Howard that connects you to this moment. When I return home, I allow this memory to pull me in and begin to type. Cookies were also a powerful incentive for Howard...

Our first Valentine's Day was spent apart. You had recently been transferred, separating us by 150 miles of twisting mountain roads. You sent flowers and three cards, which I came to expect on every significant occasion.

1. Humorous
2. Humorous and lusty
3. Romantic and sometimes scary serious.

That night we talked on the phone until very late. You playfully tried to teach me how to have phone sex, but your highly descriptive words did not call up the same feelings as your gentle hands, or the taste of your sweet exploring mouth. The only response I could manage was laughter. We eventually whispered "goodnight," and I went to sleep around midnight. We both had to be up early for work the next morning.

At around 3 AM, I was awakened when the outside motion light clicked on. It illuminated my front porch and shined through the glass door, which was across the entry hall from my open bedroom. Light, usually so welcome, reached through the lace curtain and across my bed to pry my eyes open. Every fiber of my body was on alert, listening. I hoped it was that damn stray cat again, taking feline pleasure in creeping around the neighborhood at night. But then, I heard the gate latch click softly. This was followed by the sound of slow, halting footsteps moving one after the other along the stone pathway up to the house. As they started up the ten steps to my porch, I began searching for the small pistol which I wasn't sure I could use but kept under my pillow anyway. My hands were shaking so violently I could barely hold onto it. By the time I took the safety off, there was a shadow on the other side of the door and the doorknob was moving, like someone was trying to pick the lock. That's when I found my voice, my *other* voice, and yelled like an enraged beast. "You get the hell off of my porch or I will shoot your fucking balls off." The knob stopped moving. There was a frozen moment with both of us stunned by the voice and its powerful threat. Emboldened, I shouted again. "I mean it! Get the hell out of here." The figure moved away from the door and I listened to feet retreating across the porch and down the stairs. I heard the gate latch click again and grabbed the phone to call the police. There was little they could do if I didn't have a description. After turning on all the outside lights and checking the locks, I eventually fell back asleep.

The next morning, I opened the front door and was hit in the face by a huge bouquet of red heart shaped balloons that were tied to my doorknob. There was a note dangling on a string, with a message written in familiar shaky handwriting. It read, "Happy Valentine's Day." My intruder had been the elderly neighbor, Howard, who lived next door.

That evening, I told you what had happened and shared the whole story of Howard and how our unusual friendship had developed.

I purchased the funky old house from an old lover and sometimes friend, who had repossessed it. The street was more like a one-way alley and most houses sat very close together, with little or no setback. Mine was three stories high and up a steep driveway. It had a tiny overgrown garden, a lovely, wrapped porch, and a second-story kitchen window that gazed out over the roofs of town toward snow-covered Mt. Shasta in the distance. I moved into the house with my son, Scott, and youngest daughter,

Kristen, who would soon be entering high school. By then, Kari was living with her father who would buy her cigarettes. We also brought our mixed breed dog, Boomer, who somehow made it into our car after we stopped at the animal shelter one Saturday afternoon, to *just give love.*

The move required the help of friends with trucks which, despite our best efforts, was inconvenient for neighbors on the narrow street. The need for frequent apology provided opportunities to meet many of them. A few weeks later, I noticed an older man in the yard next door whom I hadn't met. I tried to introduce myself, but he shuffled away with no eye contact, appearing to be deaf and with limited eyesight. This happened each time I encountered him.

After a few months, Boomer began acting unusually excited to go outside each morning. The reason was revealed one spring day when I sat on the porch to watch the sunrise and heard a man's voice talking sweet and low. I peeked around the corner to observe the previously silent neighbor exercising his operational vocal cords, while reaching through the back fence to pet my dog and give her treats. He wouldn't speak to me but had been seducing my dog. Boomer was experiencing no guilt over her indiscretion. There was every indication that they had established a more than neighborly relationship.

I asked another neighbor about the man who lived next door and was told that he was a "Cranky old guy who hates people and doesn't talk to anybody."

As spring sprung so did the weeds and many lovely plants that had been hidden under debris. I began to spend more time in the yard cleaning out flower beds. There were more frequent sightings of the man, who also seemed unable to resist the warmth and sunshine. If I came out while he was near my side of the yard, he would calmly and silently shuffle away. To most people, this might have been a signal to do the same. Instead, I began to sing out to his retreating backside: Good Morning neighbor!

Beautiful day! Looks like rain! Getting hot! And so on... I didn't wait for a response but sent my greeting through the air and got on with my day. His disinterest hung from hunched shoulders like rusty armor. It did a poor job of shielding him from my assault of neighborliness.

One fall afternoon, I left work early and spent some time gardening without seeing the neighbor. I eventually went inside to bake *Candy's Friend Helen's Sister's Oatmeal Chocolate Chip Cookies*, which filled the air with anticipation. My children and their friends were raised on these crunchy, chewy in-the-middle, chocolate and nut-filled, butter-laden monsters. I am still convinced that they are a health food despite the sugar because they also contain generous amounts of whole oats and walnuts.

My kitchen was on Howard's side of the house, near my back door. As I baked, I saw through the window that he had appeared outside to work along our shared wire fence. Kristen burst through the front door, pushed blond curls out of her freckled face, and squealed, "Yes! I could smell cookies for blocks." Our laughter morphed into blissful moans while sharing warm cookies. I glanced out the window again to observe our silent neighbor still crouched down in the dirt. Tossing my head in his direction, I asked, "Do you think he's smelling cookies too?" We looked at each other, grabbed a plastic bag, placed four huge cookies inside and tied it closed with a bright blue ribbon. We waited for him to leave and then went outside to hang the cookies on Howards side of the fence. After checking periodically throughout the evening, the cookies were still there when we went to bed, thoroughly disappointed. The next morning, I was preparing breakfast when I remembered to look outside. The cookies were gone. In their place, was a bundle of freshly dug flower bulbs tied together with brown twine and hung on our side of the fence. Kristen and I danced around like we had discovered a lost language. That day, when I came outside, Howard stayed on my side of the yard. He still didn't respond to my greeting but worked silently nearby.

After a short time, he stood to go and quietly but distinctly said, "You never know what you might find hanging from that fence." I sagely agreed, "You just never know." I thanked him for the Iris bulbs and he nodded somberly before going back inside.

Homemade cookies are more than sugar, flour, eggs and butter. They are also warm hands that measure, mix, shape, bake, and sometimes reach out. I would learn more about the hunger for that kind of nourishment.

Over the years, Howard and I shared cookies, jam, home-baked bread, soup, seeds, plants, books, articles, and music CDs. Most transactions took place at that wire fence, but occasionally I would come home from work and find him sitting on the garden bench at the top of my driveway, waiting for me. He had a magazine article, or music, that he thought I'd enjoy. I gradually learned about Howard through these exchanges, and he would occasionally share more than I expected. He liked to walk when it was quiet and people were asleep. He said that the police had once stopped him and asked for his identification. He refused, declaring that it wasn't illegal to walk and they had no just cause to stop him. They threw him in the patrol car, but later let him go because he was right. They made him walk several miles back home from the police station in the middle of the night. Howard said he hated "Preachers and Pigs." I suggested that saving people must be a daunting job. He responded gravely, "They are more dangerous than the sinners and the criminals." I am confident that there were more troubling stories behind this powerful emotion. He didn't offer them up and I didn't ask.

I never invited Howard inside my home. He never met my friends. I instinctively set a strong boundary and our friendship took root on the neutral piece of ground where he had surrendered to cookies. Prior to his tying balloons to my doorknob in the middle of the night, the only time that I felt uncomfortable was when he asked if I'd like to come over and watch the movie

Grumpy Old Men with him. I declined and he seemed to take it in stride.

After Valentine's Day, Howard stopped speaking to me again. He went back into hiding and pretending that I didn't exist. It occurred to me that reclusive Howard may not actually know that women experience the world differently than men. He may not realize how we constantly adjust our lives to avoid being assaulted. If he did, surely, he would never have crept into my yard and onto my porch late at night. Eventually, I walked next door to explain why I had been so frightened and angry. I wanted Howard to understand how fear can burn low, like a pilot light, until ignited into fury. With one foot in the door, I shared just two stories:

- **It was a hot summer night** when I woke to a faint scratching sound coming from my open bedroom window. I looked over to see the shape of a man's head and bent arm silhouetted against the full moon, his fingers stealthily moving around the edges, trying to pry my screen off. The police told me they suspected he was the same man who had broken in and raped a woman at knifepoint, just a few months prior. Apparently, he had a type and went on to rape and stab a third woman with a butcher knife during another full moon. Fingerprints were taken and I moved with my children across town. The immobilizing terror of that night moved with me.
- **A deep, unfamiliar, voice** on my telephone in the middle of the night accurately described where I had been. He told me what I had worn and what he would like to do to me. This man knew my name, address, and my unlisted number. He knew where I worked and that I had three kids. The FBI got involved and put a trace

on my phone. His calls stopped. They suspected a police officer. If they ever identified him, I was not notified.

I convinced myself that Howard would *want* to know about this menace that follows us through our days, and sniffs at our doors and windows at night. I was wrong. The last words Howard ever said to me were through the crack of his front door. "I never heard a voice like that before."

Valentine's Day had inspired Howard to imagine that the smiling woman at the fence might serve up more of what he hungered for. He didn't want to know about the other woman, the one with *that voice*, who also lives in this body. When she is called up, like Kali the Hindu Goddess, outrage comes with her. Howard hadn't imagined outrage being pointed in his direction, along with a handgun. He found the courage to reach for a sweet fantasy, but not the courage to accept a bitter truth about the world we live in. Howard shut the door and I never knocked again.

As time has passed, I have regretted not telling Howard more. Shame and fear still whispered in my ear back then. If I had tried to tell him, Howard may still have shut the door. But he might also have waited until I emptied myself of these stories. If that had happened, he may have found the courage to also feel outrage. I didn't know then that sharing a truth, even a difficult one, is an offering. How it is received is out of our hands.

- **I was three or four years** old when men and older boys first began to touch and coerce me to touch them, introducing me to sex much too early. I was ten or eleven when my first orgasm ocurred, with a hand over my mouth as I was being humped fully clothed against a wall at my grandmother's house. The orgasm surprised and confused me much more than the hand over my mouth, which I understood. I wanted that feeling, whatever it was, again. I was willing to be silenced for a while, but when I eventually asked for help, I was accused of making things up. It took decades for me to understand that my body was not the only magical thing I possessed.

- **I was 20 years old and newly married,** when a doctor in Ft. Smith, Arkansas, inserted his fingers into my vagina during a physical exam and began moving them slowly, in and out, while manipulating my clitoris. When I tried to sit up, red-faced, and frightened, I could see he was aroused. He held my ankles and asked, "Are you sure you want to get up?" I couldn't speak. I couldn't speak about it for years.

- **I was 32 years old** and feeling righteously independent until three drunken country boys in a pickup truck sliced up my tent and sleeping bag after discovering that I had slipped out to hide in the forest. Earlier, they had cruised through the campground at Grey Falls, and then come back after dark. I heard the truck drive in and peeked out to see that headlights were off, while voices whispered and boots scuffled. Just before that, I had heard a Cougar scream across the river, which sent chills down my spine and put me on high alert. Perhaps it saved me. I didn't camp alone again until I had a dog.

- **I was excited when *The Boss*** scheduled me to work a conference in the city. When I unlocked the door to my hotel room, I found him waiting for me, propped up and naked, in the only bed. I had small children and he knew I needed that job. Earlier that evening, at a reception, one of his associates slid a key with a suite number into my pocket, "Just in case you need a place to go." He seemed to know something I didn't. I took refuge in the bathroom until I remembered the key. As I walked with my baggage past the bed to the door, my boss slurred, "Oh Sandi, we are adults here!" It took a long time to fully comprehend the layers of power and control he had applied. Years later, he apologized while at a community event that we had both volunteered for. He was running for public office and I suspect he hoped to avoid a problem.

• **There was** *The Jogger* who saluted with three fingers touching his forehead whenever we passed, running in opposite directions. One dawn morning he hid in shrubbery and waited to slip out behind me. I leapt into the empty street as he tried to grab me just as a car magically appeared and stopped, shining its headlights on our struggle. He ran and the woman in the car drove me home. I never again ran alone at dawn or dusk.

• **I apologized for surprising** *The Friendly Fisherman*, who was standing on the riverbank when I walked down during my lunch hour. As I moved away from him, he began to follow me, ducking behind willows. When I shouted that I knew he was there, he boldly stepped out, smiling like an invitation. His smile became a confused scowl when I cut up the bank and struggled through thick brush to a parking lot. I didn't walk by the river alone for a long time.

• **On a Friday night** when my children were with their father, I worked later than usual and then went Christmas shopping. I was bone tired as I struggled with my packages through the doors of the mall and into the darkened parking lot. The previously full lot was almost empty, and my car was a far distance away. As I trudged toward it, I caught movement out of the corner of my eye and turned to see the figure of a man moving across the parking lot toward me. I instantly recognized that I fit the profile of the perfect victim –– overburdened and distracted. I squared my shoulders and quickened my pace while also reaching for the car keys in my pocket. As I got closer to my car, he got closer to me. He quickened his own pace and began talking fast, "Hey baby! Hey baby! You look like you could use some help. Let me help with those." I had just worked my key into the door when I ran out of time. Turning to confront him, I shouted angrily, "DO I KNOW YOU?" He was startled, hesitating just long enough for me to open the door. He said, "No, baby, but you want to" and lunged. He stumbled as I launched myself into the car and locked the door. He grabbed the handle and I honked the horn until he ran. I drove home shaking. The police said two women had recently been assaulted and raped in that area by someone who fit his description. I told them I could probably identify him but never got a call. I never again shopped late at night or parked away from lights after dark.

- **"It's the only time I can make it"** he said, and so I agreed to show a vacant apartment to a stranger, late one evening. I remember becoming aware that he was watching me too closely and had no questions. When I handed him the application, he dropped it and moved in front of the door. Before he could react, I banged on a wall and shouted to the neighbor who I knew was on the other side. The neighbor shouted back and passed the man on the walkway as he was hurriedly leaving. I never again showed a vacancy without pepper spray and leaving the name and number of the person I was meeting.

- **Finally, there was *The Other Boss***, also a nice guy and actual friend who I felt close to. I believed I could manage him even after he showed up at my house late one night when his wife was out of town. He seemed sheepish when I turned him away and things went back to normal. But then came the day that he drove me to evaluate a remote property and locked the gate behind us. He pulled a blanket and bottle of wine from his trunk. I needed that job too. He refused to promise that it wouldn't happen again, saying he "couldn't control his feelings." When I said I'd have to resign, he managed to control his feelings long enough to remind me that I wouldn't get unemployment benefits if I left voluntarily.

I will never forget the ice-cold feeling that moved through my body at that moment. I had been worried about his reputation and his family but came to clearly understand that he was willing to punish me and my children if I refused him. Ice became heat as anger began its slow burn. I remembered how many men seem conveniently unable to control their urge to overpower, silence, demean, coerce, assault, rape, or murder women and girls. I recalled a time in Child Welfare when an adult man raped a four-year-old girl, saying in his defense that she had "enticed" him. I thought about my friend's grandmother who was raped by a grandson when he visited her nursing home. I remembered the tense conversation with a male friend after he angrily shamed and chastised his young adult daughter for dressing in a way that he felt was too revealing. He wanted her to be safe and firmly believed she might control those kinds of men by dressing differently. The deep shame that male victims experience after being sexually assaulted must be extraordinarily shocking and painful. Women *know* it can happen and that they risk being blamed if a boy or man doesn't control himself.

I threatened to tell his wife and anyone else who would listen. We both knew that he would deny my allegations and people might not believe me, but it was too risky for him. He agreed to unemployment and let me leave. We pretended it was amicable and I took some accounts with me to begin building my own business. I had officially become an Angry Woman. But not all the time.

Years after Howard stopped speaking to me, I returned to prepare my house for sale. I noticed a stranger going in and out of his open front door and walked over to ask about him. The worker told me that Howard had died of heart failure, which I found sadly ironic. He had died in a nursing home. According to the worker, Howard told a visiting clergy who came to offer comfort, to "Go to hell." He also reported that he had been ejected from at least one other facility, because he used profanity and threw things at people who were too "officious."

My neighbor was a sick, misanthropic, and curmudgeonly old man whose primary pleasures could be counted on one hand. It was no surprise to me that when those precious things were lost, he would seek relief by offending people who imposed their goodness on him. They kept him from the privacy he craved. He had to give up his beloved cat, little cottage and garden. His vintage corvette was left behind in the garage to be inherited by a brother he seemed to have little contact with. Howard also enjoyed classical music, opera, and erotica, none of which is readily available in nursing homes.

The worker invited me inside where he was sorting things into boxes. He pulled a set of elegantly monogramed shiny gold satin sheets from a donation box and held them up with a wink. "Check these out." Original creases were intact and they were neatly encased in the custom drawstring bag they had arrived in. He asked if I wanted them and I surprised myself by accepting. They were as vintage as Howard, but slick and bright, in contrast to his craggy darkness. The golden sheets had been kept new and pristine for many years, ready for a special moment that never came. They were still waiting to be warmed by body heat and anointed with the sweet stickiness of lovemaking. When he tossed in some match books with Howard's initials, I couldn't stop myself from imagining him lighting a post-coital cigarette, like in old movies, even though I'd never seen him smoke. The man smiled broadly at me as I left, reporting over his shoulder,

"I guess that Howard guy knew how to invest in the right stocks. Turns out he was a very wealthy man."

As I walked back home, I felt my throat tightening and let my fingers wander inside the bag to feel the luxurious smoothness of the sheets. I knew that I held a tender secret. Wealth didn't keep Howard from hiding in the dark and growling at humanity. He was starving. I began to ache for him and for all the other offended and frightened men who only feel safe with women who circle them like the sun. We should all be outraged by this crippling culture.

You, Randy, were not one of those men. Each time I told you one of these stories, you listened intently and with full attention. You never once questioned the validity of my experiences, or my judgement in attempting to move as freely through my life as you did yours. When you shared my outrage, I began to believe that change was possible. Dementia cannot take away what you gave to me. Nor can it diminish my fierce love for the man that you were and still are, deep inside.

The first time you held your glass up to toast Howard was after his death. It was the same year we married. I understood that we were saluting *courage*. We continued to honor Howard's brief show of courage long after it had scuttled back into its hiding place to snuggle up with the old dependable scars that were already carved into his wounded psyche.

We were thoroughly entangled when I proposed, suggesting that we get married so I could tag onto your health insurance. You thought about it for a few days, which was your way, before holding out your hand and saying with a big grin, "Let's go for it!" I was surprised to find that we each seemed to feel more deeply committed after we married. We knew that surrendering to love guaranteed pain. You can have pain without love, but you cannot experience love without pain. We were also courageous.

My friendship with Howard began with a cookie and I did not fail to notice that our final toast to him was with a cookie.

As I finish writing these stories, I hold my wine glass up for one more toast on this Valentine's Day. I am alone now because you are sleeping across town. There is nothing to bump but air. **"Go for it!"** I say to the air. This will be my new, elegant, Valentine's Day salute. It should not be confused with, "Take what you want."

When I turn off the light and crawl between the cold sheets on my own lonely bed, I realize I am still wearing the necklace. I close my eyes and let my fingers trace the shapes of those tiny etched flowers which transport me back into our wildlife garden that now belongs to someone else. I like to imagine our mixed ashes being scattered on that same ground one day. They would sweeten the soil that nourished us and feed the Iris bulbs I planted there.

Every spring, Howard's bulbs send up thick green blades, like swords, to protectively circle the stems. These stems reach nearly three feet in height before opening their spectacular, copper-red, ruffled blossoms. Something brave and beautiful has been left behind. Another offering.

Secret Society of Naked Ladies

IT IS LATE August in Southern Oregon. You seem oblivious to the heat, but my little garden and I are both miserable. I am tired of relentless sunshine and missing the Redwoods on the Northern California coast and the cool morning mist. As I drive to your facility, I pass a small eruption of Amaryllis belladonna that seems to have sprung up overnight in a yard I pass almost daily. How could I have missed seeing these before? They are a delightful surprise as they show themselves off just when we all need a bit of chutzpah.

When I walk into the common area, I find you sitting in your usual spot on the couch. As I announce, "I saw Naked Ladies!" you glance briefly in my direction but then return your attention to the adjoining kitchen. It's lunch time and the smell of food is more tantalizing than my voice tossing words around. There was a time when you would have feigned shock and then asked for the location of these beautiful ladies.

Amaryllis belladonna is a plant species native to Cape Province, South Africa. Naked Lady is the common name and the one most people are familiar with. Aside from its spectacular flower, the most attractive thing about Amaryllis belladonna is that she has her own set of rules. Still influenced by her South African origin, Belladonna slyly begins sprouting thick green leaves in late winter or early spring when most deciduous plants are bare. Then, in late spring or early summer, when other plants are busily leafing and budding, the belladonna's leaves begin to wither and wilt, eventually creating a sad little pile of debris. If someone wasn't familiar with this trickery, they would believe the plant had mysteriously succumbed to an untimely death. But then, later in summer or early fall, depending on location, a strong stalk will vigorously push up through the nest of dried leaf remnants to proudly display an impressively large developing bud. Just when most flowering plants are winding down and preparing for fall and winter dormancy, her bud bursts open to expose a luscious pink flower that perfumes the air around it. Belladonna stands exposed, without greenery to hide her nakedness. I especially appreciate that she is not shy as she rises above the rubble of her earlier, necessary, stage of development.

This discovery of Naked Ladies in our new community brings another memory crowding into my mind. I remember you pointing and exclaiming "Naked Ladies!" with a silliness that you once manufactured just for me. Like Belladonna, this image is impossible to ignore and I find myself remembering for both of us again.

Seventeen or eighteen years ago, we were driving past an old Victorian house in Eureka, California, when you hit the brakes and pulled your truck over to the side of the road. You pointed across the street toward the house and asked excitedly, "What are those?" I saw that the yard was completely covered with Amaryllis belladonna in full bloom. The bulbs had been allowed to naturalize and spread throughout a large area that had once been a lawn. It was an unexpected and dazzling display of soft color. When I informed you they were "Naked Ladies," you chuckled and then said somberly, with one eyebrow raised, "I have always admired naked ladies."

I was just as intrigued when I first heard that name. I have met people who find the emphasis on female nakedness offensive. They make me tired. Others assume she is called "Lady" entirely because of her pink color. They would be wrong. Belladonna itself means "beautiful woman" in Italian. Amaryllis is a Greek female name meaning to 'shine', or 'sparkle', which Belladonna certainly does. In Greek mythology, the beautiful maiden, Amaryllis, fell in love with Alteo, a handsome shepherd boy who loved flowers. It is difficult to imagine a common name more fitting than Naked Lady.

I confess to wondering what it might feel like to remove the clothes from my middle-aged body and dance among these lovely pink ladies to celebrate our proud nakedness together. The ridiculous image makes me grin. Like most young girls, I was encouraged to quiet my "dopey thoughts" and mold my body to please others, both in appearance and service. According to Alice Walker, "resistance" is *The Secret of Joy.* I have come to agree. When we resist suppression and begin to reveal what our hearts and minds have to say, the words taste especially sweet on our tongues. We are lighter when we hand back the shame, and happier dancing to the music that moves us. This is who we were all meant to be.

You enjoyed the creatively imposed characteristics that I assigned Amaryllis belladonna and immediately declared Naked Ladies to be your new favorite flower. You said that they represented your kind of woman. Before we drove away from the uproarious display, I teasingly asked, "Which Naked Lady is your favorite?" You responded, "That would have to be my unruly Sandi." It was a good answer. If you also imagined me dancing among them, you kept it to yourself.

For a short time, "Naked Lady" was our code for women who show us, even briefly, who they really are. Our Naked Ladies aren't interested in silencing or limiting anyone else. They simply stop asking for permission to participate. They don't apologize for taking up space. They don't smile when they are angry or nod if they disagree. They share their thoughts when they have something to say.

I recall a time that friends introduced us to a wonderfully unrestrained woman. It wasn't long before you leaned over to me and quipped, "SHE is a Naked Lady." It turned out to be an easily misunderstood comment that we learned to keep to ourselves.

You were an accidental Feminist who sincerely believed that *all people* deserve the same freedom of choice, benefits of citizenship, representation where decisions are made, equal opportunities and compensation, along with an unquestioned right to the safety and general respect that you, a straight, white man of stature, enjoyed. Your willingness to examine your own privilege and deeply imbedded bias also set you apart from most other men I have been close to. You had done things that you were deeply ashamed of and were willing to examine those also. You voluntarily attended a seminar on gender bias because you wanted to understand better. One of our more serious disagreements was over a blatantly sexual joke you made to your adolescent son about Girl Scouts and their cookies. You later expressed regret for this and admitted to being a "work in progress." We all are. There was still work to do when dementia took your brain hostage. I still take some comfort in knowing that you did not continue to ignore an entire person in favor of her parts because of willful ignorance or disrespect.

In the early stages of FTD, as dementia destroyed insight and impulse control, I made a choice. I could laugh with you or be angry and embarrassed by your behaviors. I experienced all three, but mostly I laughed with you. I even laughed when you began to greet our women friends by cupping their breasts and chortling delightedly, "Are those boobies?" I put a note on our front door before gatherings: "Warning! All breasts entering here are at risk of being fondled." Friends who couldn't set aside their discomfort, rightly stopped coming over. Most rose to the occasion and laughed with you, responding, "These are MY boobies" while brushing aside your hands, along with your demented giggle. There were even hurt feelings when you left one friend out. She was heard to ask, "What's the matter with my boobies?" Your male friends just stood by, watching with envy. I love these people.

Before FTD, if I had an evening out with women friends, you usually wanted to hear what we had talked about. You knew we talked openly about actual feelings and things not measured on a score board. We wove our way through work, relationships, community, books, family, politics, spirituality, sexuality, joy, grief, and sometimes even men. Our opinions and thoughts interested you.

After you became ill, a group of close women friends that we dubbed SPAT (our first initials) occasionally allowed you to join us. On those nights, we became SPAT+R. SPATR ended when my need for respite became stronger than your need for socializing. I always felt a little guilty about that, but I needed to take care of my own sanity.

The Booby Grabbing Phase of dementia passed without jail time. However, you still seem especially pleased when women are present. You once told me that you always had girlfriends, even in kindergarten. It is the same now that you are in memory care. I try not to compete.

Within a week of moving to your memory care facility, I would walk in and find you sitting on the couch with an elderly woman on either side. One believed you were her son. The other was clearly infatuated, installing herself as your first Memory Care Girlfriend. In this story she will be Louise.

LOUISE WAS YOUNGER than most women in the facility, but not nearly as young as you. So far, nobody has been as young as you. Louise would sit very close to you and scowl at me when I pulled up a chair or leaned down to kiss your cheek. Her curly gray hair framed a round expressive face. Her skin was smooth, with few wrinkles, and her soft feminine body was still mobile. Like you, she produced few words, so there was no pressure to communicate in that way. You mostly ignored her but also didn't push her away. It seemed to feel good when Louise sat too close.

Like you, Louise was playful. She would randomly pat your

head or your crotch, tickle your ribs, and seductively sway to music when someone turned it on. I always greeted her warmly and she would sometimes surprise me by tweaking my nipples, a cagy smile on her face. These were glimpses of who Louise might have been before dementia. Sometimes her expression would quickly change to dismay without an obvious reason. The corners of her mouth would begin to draw down, like little fingers of memory were tugging at them. When this happened, she never hid her face like she might have before dementia. Instead, she kept steady eye contact while soft tears slid down her cheeks. She didn't wipe them away but just let them be what they were... wet and forlorn. These little storms were mercifully brief and Louise would soon forget what had made her sad. The corners of her mouth would suddenly turn up and she would begin to smile again. Dementia allowed her to be as unapologetically exposed as your favorite flower. When it occurred to me that Louise was a *Naked Lady,* I resurrected our code name for women who drop their masks and stop pretending, even if only for a moment.

I knew that Louise spent time in your room watching movies with you. Other residents also wandered in and out, which you seemed ambivalent to. During that period, you were still refusing to lie in your bed, preferring to sleep in your recliner instead. Sometimes I would find Louise's socks, or a blouse on your floor. After I found her socks in your bed one day, staff apprehensively admitted to me that she had been leaving her own bed in the middle of the night, making her way down the hall and climbing into yours, which was next to your chair. One of the caregivers had once observed you getting up from your chair to carefully cover her with your quilt, patting it gently into place around her before returning to your recliner. They didn't want to tell me about this because they were afraid it would upset me. The image of you tucking Louise in certainly did bring tears to my eyes, but not for the reasons they imagined. You are still tender and kind, and neither of you slept alone on those nights.

While you still have a gleam in your eye from time to time, I feel grateful that your advanced illness, along with your medications, has eliminated sexual urges in your body. This would present another gnarly layer of difficulty for us all. You are still young and strong while your Memory Care Girlfriends are not.

Louise is now in a wheelchair and can no longer walk down the hall during the night. Nor does she sway to music, tickle your ribs, or pat your crotch. She shows no interest in you. You have both moved further inward and I seem to be the only one who is saddened by this. The vacant space next to you has been filled by your second and current Memory Care Girlfriend. I will call her Sue.

SUE CONFUSES YOU with her dead husband. She is a lovely and warm person with a bright smile. Sue is thin and her hair is still mostly dark with a bit of gray weaving through. She is in a wheelchair but maneuvers it with skill. When I ask, "How are you today?" she grins and responds, "I am wonderful." Unlike you and Louise, Sue still has language. She often makes the same mistake I do and sends too many nonsensical words in your direction.

Some people are troubled by her obsession with you. Staff is repeatedly needing to redirect her because she isn't eating well and passing her food to you, which causes diarrhea. She prefers to stay by your side in the room where you take your meals. You don't eat in the dining room because they could never fully break your habit of taking other peoples' food. Sue brings you hers. As with Louise, I suspect this is a glimpse into Sue's previous life.

Again, you seem mostly disinterested in Sue. You casually lean over to look around her when she plants herself in front of you, blocking your view of the TV. But you don't push her away. You were once observed curiously squeezing her thin arm up and down with one hand, like testing an avocado for ripeness. That was the day that she took her blouse off and tried to climb out of her wheelchair and onto your lap. Someone said you look very much like her husband did. They also said he was selfish and cruel.

For all the reasons that women refuse to leave uncaring or violent men, I am told that Sue remained with him until he died. When she might have had an opportunity to create a different life for herself, Dementia took his place of dominance. If she now believes you are her changed, gentler husband, what is the harm? I make it clear to staff that I hope she won't be shamed for this, especially since you still seem able to take care of yourself. If she strokes your hand too much, you put it into your pocket. If she rubs your leg or whispers in your ear too long, you gently move her wheelchair aside to stand and walk about.

One day, Sue was not in the common area when I arrived. You and I were sitting side-by-side on the couch with our fingers laced together when she rolled in and discovered me there. She frantically wheeled toward us, murmuring while quickly closing the distance. As always, I greeted her with a smile. She seemed to relax until her eyes were drawn to your hand and saw it linked with mine. A look of renewed alarm spread across her face and she reached out to grab your other hand, which was lying empty in your lap. Your expression never changed as you quickly shoved your free hand into your pocket. She tugged on your left forearm with both hands, trying with all her might to pull it from its hiding place. I could see your muscles tense while your hand didn't budge. You were still quite strong.

I successfully pushed back the smug smile that tried to creep onto my face, but I couldn't subdue the triumph surging in my chest. I was willing to share, but you were not. I felt admiration for Sue's courage in reaching for what she wanted, but also felt selfish pleasure in retaining my status of #1. As I prepared to leave, I gave her a big hug and whispered, "Welcome to the Naked Ladies Club." She responded, "Bye, bye."

The Secret Society of Naked Ladies is now a thing. It is my thing. I have inducted both Sue and Louise into my club without their permission. I don't know if they were as transparent before dementia, but I am glad to know them now. They are unaware of the honor I have bestowed.

I am now remembering other women who influenced me and whose stories you enjoyed. The kind of pretending that Naked Ladies reject is not about hair style, clothing selection, or even the momentary politeness we all engage in. It is about firmly discarding the carefully planted belief that her ambitions, thoughts, ideas, or voice are unacceptable. Naked Ladies, at some point in their lives, reject that these must be hidden or altered to be loved. Some of the most dangerous participants of the patriarchal culture that imposes these values, are women who shun and shame other women for stepping out of compliance. They cannot yet imagine a life where mutual respect and responsibility for one another provides opportunities for mutual satisfaction. We are all afraid.

It is important to more deeply explore the ways men and boys are also trained to bend to cultural standards that include dominance. As women continue to nurture their strengths, and men to acknowledge their vulnerabilities, we will hold each other up.

Memories of other Naked Ladies are now dancing in my mind like fireflies on a summer night. When I get home, I will scatter words into my computer so they will also fly like blessings into the night. I want to reintroduce you to these women who shaped me and who I don't want to forget.

MOLLY WAS NEARING 70 when I met her. You met her just a year or two before she died, when she was in her 80s. She was the matriarch of a group of women who called themselves Carrie Nation, in honor of the 6' tall, radical member of the Women's Christian Temperance movement, which preempted Prohibition. Carrie was known for smashing up bars with a hatchet, leaving shattered whiskey bottles and scattering drunken men all over Kansas. Our group honored her rebellious, fiery spirit and shared her dislike of drunken, irresponsible, and abusive men. We also shared numerous bottles of wine at these gatherings which demonstrated a different sentiment about drunken women. In our defense, not one person in this group was known to shirk responsibilities or abuse another person while drinking wine. I'd also never met women who were so noisy about things that I had been taught to be quiet about. Wine loosens tongues and amplifies voices.

I didn't realize Molly was close to my mother's age when she first shared some of her story while we sat in a hot tub chatting with other women friends. My mother had never allowed herself to enjoy such an evening. Molly was a graduate of Smith College and later became an architect. She married another architect, Alan, whom she met at UC Berkley. Most women during that era didn't go to college, let alone acquire advanced degrees and become professionals in a field dominated by men. People would frequently walk into their office, where her name was also on the door, but still assume she was the secretary. When Alan introduced her, he would include her qualifications as a business partner and spouse. She said she was amused that their responses were often more confused than apologetic. She had also worked in the city's Building and Planning Department during a time when coworkers were mostly men. Her challenges to be heard in meetings reminded me of Ruth Bader Ginsberg, who was persistent while refusing to be loud and angry. She sometimes changed minds by teaching... like a pre-school teacher. Like Ruth Bader Ginsberg, Molly rarely lashed out in public, believing it to be counterproductive when wanting to be heard. I took note as she demonstrated who she was. I had never met anyone like her.

Molly was a true 'no fuss' woman. She wore no makeup, little jewelry, and kept her hair very short. After she discovered that women's hair salons charged four times as much as barber shops, she began going to the barber for cuts.

Molly and Alan had education, ample resources, and medical insurance that offered them choices not everyone enjoys. Despite this, she elected to receive her routine medical care at the public clinic, which primarily served low-income people. Molly was convinced that the quality of care would improve for everyone if we all did the same.

One of my favorite Molly stories was when she was treated for breast cancer in her late 50s. She was recuperating in the hospital after a single mastectomy when a nurse came in and began measuring her wound and chest area, all the while reassuring her that things would "look the same as before." Molly wondered out loud "why things should look the same when they were now very different?" The nurse seemed confused, so Molly simply asked why she was measuring her. The nurse seemed relieved to explain that they would be making a prosthetic breast and a special bra for it to reside in. Molly was thoughtful for a moment and then asked, "Will it also feed my grandchild?"

Molly never received the fake breast and she never tried to hide the obvious fact that one side of her blouse hung flat and loose. She has been gone for over 20 years now. I wish I had known her as well as others who have many more stories to tell. It was her clarity and willingness to do what she believed to be right, which inspired me to open my own mind in ways I had not previously considered.

I suspect Molly would find it unnecessary, perhaps even ridiculous, to be inducted into my secret society. I have appointed her anyway and she hasn't objected so far.

LAURA LEE WAS born in 1904. Her mother described a "helmet of red hair" when she arrived. It didn't perform well as a protector but captured attention throughout her life. It was still red in her 70s, with the help of Flame Red hair dye. Even at that age she still sparked an occasional lingering glance from men on the street. This was despite a slightly crooked and flattened nose that had been broken by one of her husbands. Another husband dragged her through a field by her hair, causing a bald spot that was visible for many months. Laura's black eyes and broken nose slowly healed and her bald spot eventually filled in beneath the hats she wore to cover it. Her teeth, however, never grew back after they were knocked out by a different husband. Nobody called the police, and the replacements went into a jar every single night for the rest of her life.

Laura Lee was my grandmother. She had an 8th grade education and was the eldest of three girls and six boys. I was twenty when she confided to me that she and her sisters had all been "loved" by their father when they were little girls. 'Love' is the word she whispered with furtive glances around her living room where just two of us sat. Other verbs and adjectives were available to her by then, but she would not allow her mouth to say them.

Uncles sometimes participated. Cousins and brothers were instructed how to "*do it,*" and reportedly took turns. This horrifying dominance and misuse of female children had been passed down for generations on both sides of her family. Of course, the boys were also children, and many grew up to be misogynistic, drunken, or otherwise incomplete men who were unable to have healthy relationships with women. Laura Lee learned to surrender –– first her body and then her dreams. She began to want what men wanted and believed she might be loved and protected in exchange. It never worked out that way. I was told that she had been married many times and have found records to verify three. Not all unions were licensed.

Laura became pregnant when she was 15 and delivered the baby, Harold, at 16. She had Winifred at 17. She described how dumbfounded she was when the doctor first told her she was going to have a baby. She laughed her crusty smokers laugh, saying she had asked him, "How is it going to get out?" He responded, "The same way it got in."

As she aged, it became more difficult for Laura to attract the brutal and unpredictable kind of man that had always excited her. Men like her father.

In 1942, at the age of 39, Laura had responded to the call from Uncle Sam for women to serve their country by doing essential work previously performed by men who were shipping overseas to fight Hitler and the Japanese. She was inspired by pictures of 'Rosie the Riveter' with her clear eyes, muscled arm, and lipstick. Rather than a factory, Laura applied to be a streetcar operator in San Francisco. Instead, she was assigned a city bus that drove through Alameda and Oakland and then across the Bay Bridge to San Francisco, several times a day. She told me that the remaining male drivers, too old or disabled for war, smirked and made fun of her when she began training. Many women still didn't drive cars then, let alone huge buses.

When the war ended, the government reversed public media messages. Women began to hear that they should go back to their kitchens. Mothers were warned that if they didn't stop working, their children would become delinquents. The well designed and government funded Lanham Child Care Centers, where children were cared for, nourished, and educated during the war, were gradually defunded and dismantled, making it especially difficult for women with young children to continue working outside the home after the war. Laura Lee's children were already grown and there would be no soldier-husband returning to her. And she had never particularly enjoyed kitchens.

Laura was one of the rebellious women who refused to relinquish their jobs to returning soldiers who fought in World War II. She said she hoped any punishment she received would "hurt less than a fist." She had always worked but never received such a consistent and comfortable wage, or benefits.

Laura ignored Uncle Sam's coercions and kept on driving

her bus. Even after some co-workers revived their disapproving attitudes toward her, she kept her head down and showed up every day. She vowed to drive until someone took her keys away. That never happened. Laura continued to make a livable wage, receive sick leave, paid vacations, and affordable health care until she retired at age 65 on a decent pension. She also received numerous safety awards over the years, which silenced those demeaning old jokes about *women drivers*.

When we were small, my brother and I called her "Grandma Drive-a-bus." By that time, she had stopped marrying dangerous men and was driving her huge city bus back and forth across the Oakland Bay Bridge.

I vividly remember climbing up the steep steps of her bus to be transported to 'The City' with tall buildings that could be seen like a magical kingdom in the misty distance. I don't remember why I spent the night with her but I do remember being awakened very early, when it was cold and dark. I remember our feet echoing as we walked through the cavernous bus terminal and that I attached myself to her like a barnacle. I watched closely as she performed her tasks, filling out paperwork and moving things in and out of her locker. She introduced me to a few other drivers, all men, then clasped my hand firmly. I followed her lead as we straightened our shoulders and walked proudly together out of the building and into the cold fog. There was a job to do. We marched across a vast parking lot to the place where her bus was waiting. While the engine warmed up, she strolled down the aisle checking seats on both sides. She made sure I had my books and snacks and settled me onto the passenger seat directly behind her before she took her own, supremely important place, in the driver's seat.

My grandmother was a petite woman who wore her trim uniform with pride. She was quick with a smile and would jump nimbly down to assist elderly or disabled passengers and mothers with children, ensuring that they climbed or descended the steps of her bus safely. I was especially awed by how confidently she maneuvered the massive vehicle through traffic.

The first pre-dawn route started in Alameda and then went through downtown Oakland. When we stopped to pick up early groups of passengers, I saw mostly black women who carried large cloth satchels and wore low-heeled shoes that often had the backs broken down. Grandma greeted most of them by name and introduced me with great pride. They oohed and awed, patted my cheeks and touched my blond curls, telling me how pretty I was and that I was lucky to have a grandmother like mine. I believed them. Some brought little gifts to Laura and she would ask about their sore feet and their families. Women greeted each other at every stop and the cavernous bus began to fill with the sound of voices talking and laughing. I will never forget how different they were from passengers later in the day. They grew quiet when the sun began to rise behind us and worked to penetrate the blanket of fog that covered San Francisco Bay. Its light did not yet reveal how dizzyingly high above the water we were as we traveled over the Bay Bridge that first time. Most of these women left the bus with, "Thank you!" or "You have a nice day now!"

Later that morning, we collected and then ejected serious-faced men in suits and shiny shoes. They carried newspapers and briefcases. Some responded when Laura said, "Good Morning!" Most did not. Then there were sets of women in lipstick and high-heeled shoes, chatting about lunching and shopping 'in the city'. Most parroted "Good Morning." I seemed to be the only one on the bus who noticed when the fog lifted and how sunlight began to sparkle and dance on the waves below. The women were talking and most men were reading newspapers. They missed the ferry boats. Nobody around me seemed to notice Alcatraz Island in the far distance, with its prison standing at grim attention. They didn't watch tugboats pulling a ship out from under the bright orange Golden Gate Bridge that also stretched a huge distance across two pieces of land so people could drive over water. I couldn't imagine being so old that I stopped noticing such amazing things. Some said, "Have a nice day," to my grandmother as they stepped off her bus. I don't remember anyone saying, "Thank you." But it was a long time ago and I was very young.

The most memorable sounds that have remained with me from that day are the voices of the black women who boarded the bus in the cold dark of pre-dawn. I learned that many of these women worked for wealthy white families in San Francisco. The single face I see most clearly is of a young black girl standing in the darkness with a crying baby on her hip, waiting for their mother to kiss them goodbye before she climbed onto the bus and left them behind. The mother explained to my grandmother that the "baby was sick again." She had to go to work. Grandma told me she worked taking care of other people's children. The girl, who was around nine or ten, stayed home from school to care for her baby brother.

I later came to understand that children from poor and under-educated families, whether in rural areas or inner cities, do not usually struggle in school because they are 'stupid' or 'lazy.' I also learned that staying home to care for young children is still not a choice every woman, or man, has within their reach. Most of us work to survive rather than to fulfill ourselves. Fulfillment often comes from other sources and it is easier to explore these when one's basic needs are met because you are compensated fairly and respected as a human being.

As a child, I remember there was usually a drunken uncle sleeping in the basement, or on the couch at Laura's house. These were adult men who were also broken by childhood sexual abuse and alcohol. *Laura Lee and her job took care of them too.*

When I was older, I could glimpse the depression that would slide in and try to crush my grandmother's confidence and resolve. During those times, she would sit smoking and coughing in front of the TV for an entire weekend. She consumed nothing but Frito corn chips, Milk of Magnesia, quinine water, and bad coffee. Her reading material alternated between beauty magazines and the bible. I marveled at how she was able to pull herself together when it was important enough. When Laura walked out the front door to go to church or to drive her bus, her red hair was styled and sprayed, cheeks carefully rouged, and bright red lipstick applied. Punctual and impeccably dressed, she closed the door on utter filth. There were piles of newspapers on the floor and stuff on every surface; dried dishes in the sink; mice and their droppings in drawers and cupboards, and nests of dog hair in corners. Neighbors routinely complained to authorities about the stench of dog shit piling up in her overgrown yard. Curtains were always drawn. Laura had been taught to keep secrets, and to believe that therapy was for self-absorbed wealthy women. Another carefully placed tether to discourage her from thinking or learning too much about herself.

My grandmother never baked me a cookie and certainly never sewed or knitted anything for me to hide in the back of my drawer. She often forgot my birthday. Yet, I thought she was amazing. I will never forget that sunny day when I was five or six years old, and she drove me to 'The City' in her magical bus, across a spectacular bridge that stretched over San Francisco Bay. I saw a fascinating place of water and light, intriguing people, noises, and smells that I would be drawn back to as a young adult seeking my first real job in a bank at the age of 18.

It is because of the time when she showed her muscle, like Rosie the Riveter, that I have inducted Grandma Drive-a-Bus into my Secret Society of Naked Ladies. Laura Lee became entirely qualified when she stood above the dark debris of her life and refused to release the steering wheel that provided choices, pride, and a measure of security. She also got up off the couch when she could barely feed herself, to drive her bus. She once told me that she never stopped craving the attention of men. Even so, she sunk her false teeth into an opportunity that greatly reduced their power over her.

When I told you this story and showed you pictures of Laura Lee, your only comment was made after a thoughtful moment of silence: "Your family is really interesting."

WINIFRED IS 95. She is also an angry woman. But not all the time. She loves children if they like her too. She is also happy with adults if she feels admired and in control. During those times she is delightful, funny, creative, and kind. As she ages and becomes more dependent on others, she has more difficulty managing her anger, which will erupt without warning. I think of this line from a movie whose name I can't remember: "You just can't love someone with that much hurt inside." I am here to say, "You can, but it is dangerous."

Today, when I walk into the dining room of her assisted living facility, I see that Winifred's eyes have narrowed and her lips are clamped tightly together. Her thin, age-spotted hands grip each other to stop the shaking that has begun. As I walk toward her table, I begin to imagine smoke coming out of her ears like Yosemite Sam, a favorite cartoon character from my childhood. Winifred is my mother. This image was a coping mechanism when I was young and learning to laugh at things that weren't funny.

Now, she begins to escalate into one of her "fits" as she calls them. These tremors begin in her legs or hands before progressing to whole body shaking that sometimes causes her legs to kick into the air. Today, when she almost kicks herself out of her wheelchair, one of the care staff helps me to wheel her back to her room.

As with most of us, fear is the root of Winifred's rage. However, rage is the source of her strength. It is a dilemma. She is terrified when she is unable to control her environment or the people around her.

While her tremors don't always have an identifiable trigger, this episode did. I learned that a "dummy" who also lives in her facility, had wandered into the dining room before Winifred arrived. She dared to move pieces of a puzzle which Winifred had set up on a spare table for everyone's enjoyment. Winifred was sincere in this effort. However, the other reason, the one she could not acknowledge, was that she wanted people to appreciate her efforts and work the puzzle with her. After this mutinous betrayal, she attempted to hold back her anger but it retaliated by assaulting her nervous system. Rage will make its presence known, one way or another.

Winifred was unable to fix the puzzle because she started shaking and couldn't hold the pieces still enough to place them. She was also unable to hold her fork, or drink her tea without spilling, which embarrassed her and upset her even more, causing more shaking. Back in her room, she had trouble calming down. I tried to get her to eat some yogurt because low blood sugar sometimes contributes. She refused and we gave her half of an Ativan which made her fall asleep. The shaking stopped.

My mother doesn't mean to be a narcissist. She wasn't born this way. I was 17 and sitting in a college psychology class when I first heard that word. When I learned more about narcissistic personality disorders, a neon sign began flashing in my brain, "MOTHER, MOTHER" with bright yellow lights. I learned that there are necessary and healthy stages of narcissism during childhood development, but if a child's needs are not met because of either overindulgence, or neglect, they can develop what is call a *pathological* narcissism which is a broad term that covers multiple behaviors. It is a developmental wound that never seems to heal. If you add serious abuse, the trauma digs a deeper hole. Later, when I got some counseling, I was able to set boundaries that allowed me to have a relationship with my mother.

Winifred has never been able to fill the cavernous hole in her soul. Her hunger for validation demands to be fed whenever she feels powerless, or anything less than special. When she doesn't get enough, anger fills the empty space and punishment strikes like lightening. When she feels safe and in control, she is utterly delightful. I have begun to question my wisdom in refusing to lie to her, like others do, to avoid upsetting her. Maybe it would be easier on us both. I suspect I have been punishing her with truth that she cannot manage.

For the first two or three years after you and I became a couple, Winifred would refuse to speak directly to you. Out of the blue she would declare to the air: "Degrees don't make anyone smart." (She was very intelligent but never went to college.) Or: "Environmentalists are idiots." (You would offset politically driven misinformation when you could.) She would studiously ignore you if you walked into the room and said, "Good Morning, Winifred." She would also talk *about* you while in your presence. Once, she disgustedly asked me, "How can he stand that long hair?" I suggested that she "Ask him," pointing out that you were three feet away. She stomped off and you winked at me. Unlike me, you just let her be. We also had an agreement that you would not step in when my mother or my brother insulted me, unless it got nasty. In that case we would leave. You broke that agreement one time when she greeted me with a disgusted look and said, "I know you have nice clothes somewhere. Why don't you wear them?" You responded before I had a chance, saying, "She looks GREAT. You might want to get your eyes checked Winifred."

Her hostility toward you ended after she had a mild stroke, but it wasn't because of a brain reset. We still lived in California at that time and you had a weeklong business meeting in Oregon. I asked you to stop by the hospital and take her some flowers on your way back home. You smiled and asked, "Do you really think that's a good idea?" I replied that I did, but reminded you that her reaction was, as always, up to her. You agreed to do this for me because I was unable to get away from work. When you returned home that evening, you told me that when you walked into her room, she was talking with someone who had their back to you. She glanced up, grinned broadly, and said very loudly, **"HERE IS MY *FAVORITE* SON-IN-LAW."** You described literally turning around to see who was behind you. It was over. You finally won her heart by bringing her flowers in the hospital where others could see how loved she was. You could have been Ted Bundy and it wouldn't have mattered. We chuckled over that for years. I have always been a little slow figuring some things out.

Winifred can't hear now, but she hates the hearing aids that would assist her. She has heart failure, kidney failure, Addison's disease, and recurring bowel blockages that have required surgeries that she wasn't expected to survive. She has severe osteoporosis which results in repeated hairline fractures and recurring pain. It is enough to make anybody cranky. The episodic tremor also hovers in the background, waiting for something to flip its switch and further complicate an already difficult situation. She has gradually lost the use of her legs, requiring a wheelchair to safely get around. She hates that too, and often rebels by standing up on her own, which results in repeated falls and trips to the ER for stitches and scans.

One thing I can count on is that when she arrives in the ER, she will become hilariously entertaining, reveling in the attention of a fresh audience as she gets evaluated, stitched, and bandaged. There is mutual chemistry here where everyone needs a break from pain and despair. They say, "She is a gem," or "I want to take her home." I smile and respond, "Wouldn't that be fun!" I laugh louder than I should. She has managed to get out for another adventure, yet I know that it probably wasn't purposeful falling, but rebellious standing.

These ER visits remind me of when I was a young and she would talk very loudly to me when we were in public places like grocery stores. She wasn't really talking to me. She was talking to get the attention of people around us who might be enticed to engage with her. It was a performance. One day I asked her just as loudly, "Why do you talk this way when people are around?" She became very angry and I learned to more quietly accept that I had a different mother in different settings. She became distrustful of my loyalty.

My dad (who eventually adopted us), has now died and she misses him terribly. During the last couple of years before he passed, he would repeatedly tell me (when we managed to get a moment of privacy), "She isn't the same. I can't say anything without her getting mad." We agreed that maybe this was because of the stroke, even though it had been several years. I didn't suggest that old age may have made it more difficult for her to pretend.

Winifred often tells me that she doesn't want to be here anymore, and then waits for a response. I once sympathized that "I understand." This wasn't what she wanted to hear. She told others that I "wanted her to die." After I suggested putting her end-of-life wishes in writing with an Advanced Directive, and learning about Hospice, she told my brother that I belonged to some kind of "death club." She says she is "Ready to go" but she's not packing. She keeps going to doctors for prescriptions, procedures and cures. She is angry when they are unable to give her one. One specialist recently patted her hand and gently said, "Unfortunately, we still have no cure for old age." On the way home, she raged that they "just give up on old people." There is some truth to this so I did not ask her, "When will it be time to stop fighting?"

Each day is an unhappy day. If someone comes to visit, they do not stay long enough. If they bring gifts, their selection is often thoughtless or useless. If they try to help, they are taking over. If they come to share lunch with her in the dining room, it is because they get a free meal. She gossips with care givers and pits them against each other. She buys their loyalty with cash and then outs them if they don't remain devoted. She lies to her son about her daughter, and lies to her daughter about her son, hoping to inspire anger on her behalf. It makes her feel loved when someone is willing to fight for her. She is validated when someone shares her disgust. She accuses people of stealing... remaining convinced even after finding an item that she was sitting on, or otherwise misplaced. It is not an easy life. She does not have dementia.

In June of 2001, Winifred and I were driving through Denver to attend a luncheon for my daughter Kristen, her youngest granddaughter, who was getting married in a few days. I was behind the wheel and Mom was next to me with the map. She had not been back to the city where she was born since she left at age 15 when she was put on a train to join her mother, Laura Lee, who had followed a new man to California. As we came off the freeway, Winifred accidentally directed me to go right instead of left, which took us several miles in the opposite direction of where we were supposed to be. This was before GPS. When we finally realized what we had done, she threw the map down and began to berate herself for being stupid. This was also something I was familiar with and I braced myself for a rough afternoon. As I prepared to turn around, she leaned forward in her seat and pointed at an old brick school building, saying that she thought she had gone to school there. It used to be a town called Barnum before Denver swallowed it up. I asked her if she thought she could find where she lived, but she said firmly that it couldn't possibly be there any longer. When I asked why, she hesitated and then told me they had lived in an old railroad car. I knew they were very poor but didn't know that.

I drove into the neighborhood behind the school and she was able to pick out a residence that she said used to be a country store. It didn't take much imagination to see what she was talking about. The building had a double door entry under a section of roof that extended out, looking like it may have had a gas pump at one time. There were benches on either side of the doors. She became very animated as she remembered the names of the people who ran it and how she occasionally walked there as a child to pick up something for her Grandmother Middleton, who had raised her. With this landmark identified, I asked if she could pick out the place where the railroad car had been, and she had me drive back and forth a few times before directing me up an alley lined with garages and sheds. She said there used be a field there. We finally stopped behind a strange little house built in a U-shape. She thought it might have been there. As we got out of the car to look, I pointed out to her that the middle of the house looked a bit like a box car that had been placed on a foundation, with wings added. She eyed it carefully, nodded, and climbed back into the car. We sat quietly for a long time. She didn't say another word until we got to the luncheon — very late.

My mother once described herself with just two words, "big" and "ugly." She had been tall and willowy during an era when girls were supposed to be small and delicate. Childhood pictures show her with hunched shoulders and looking down. She had thick, auburn red hair, and a round freckled face that still goes from pale white to beet red in a flash. There is one adorable photo where she is looking toward the camera with her head tilted to one side. She appears to be around two or three years old. I have a picture of her standing in a similar way at her 90th birthday celebration.

When Winifred was born, her grandmother, Anna Middleton, and the local doctor were the only ones attending. Nobody mentioned Winifred's father, Otto, but in those days, childbirth was women's business. She said once that he had "gone to war," but the only conflict I could find during 1921 was the US occupation of Haiti. Wherever he was, it appears that he did not return to Laura Lee and her babies. My mother has no memory of him and was warned to run if he ever reappeared, because he would take her into "white slavery."

It was reportedly a long labor and Winifred wasn't breathing when she finally arrived. The doctor was said to have wrapped the blue and limp newborn in a towel and tossed it on a chair, saying, "Just as well." They were poor 'white trash.' It was my great-grandmother Anna, who picked Winifred up, cleared out her airway and revived her. Her grandmother would be the only one to provide her with a measure of stability. She also punished with a fury and turned her head when terrible things were done. Laura Lee's first child, my Uncle Harold, was coddled, spoiled, and taught to use and abuse women. He later spent some years in San Quentin (I never knew for what) and seemed unable or unwilling to hold a job. He attached himself to a string of women who would take care of him for a while and then return to his mother in between. When he neared middle-age, Harold found a kind woman who didn't seem to tire of taking care of him. They both took care of my grandmother after she became bedridden in her last years.

As a child, Winifred would mostly see her mother when she came back home to recover from her latest failed relationship. Once back on her feet, Laura would run off again with renewed hope for a bright future that was always packaged in the form of a new man, who turned out to be remarkably like the previous one. Laura had also been taught to believe at an early age that her only real currency was her body. The boys were taught the same thing about the value of girls. They were also taught that it was manly to dominate and take what they wanted. These beliefs and values have been passed down through many generations.

Winifred believes she was around five or six years old the first time her grandfather, the Black Irishman, raped her... like he had her mother. He continued to rape her repeatedly throughout her childhood and held her down for other male family members. She told me he "raped all the little girls in the family" but was meaner to her because she got mad. She confided this to me when she was 80 years old, shaking as she did so. This is when I began to understand and forgive her.

Winifred was neighborly and friendly. Many people liked her, including my childhood friends. But if she got too close and became vulnerable, the relationship would be destroyed by an unforgivable act like a careless comment, or lack of adequate appreciation for a kindness she had extended. Sometimes it was because of a gift she wanted back, saying they had not understood it was a loan. She wanted to be generous but had difficulty giving up stuff because she didn't own anything as a child. If it weren't for dad, I could imagine her on one those Hoarder shows, suffocating under piles of useless possessions during her elder years.

Winifred has never trusted men or women. But men have power. She met Bernard (the only dad I would know) in high school when she was 16 or 17 while living in Oakland with her mother and her mother's current man. She told me that she returned from school one day to discover her mother had moved out, leaving a note that she would send for her later. She left no money. The Landlady fed her and let her stay in their basement so she was able to continue school for several months. She described washing her body and her clothes in a laundry sink. She eventually landed a part-time job after school and was able to rent a furnished room. She was the first woman in her family to receive a high school diploma. She told me that Bernie was the first boy who ever liked her. He was very tall and painfully thin, wore wire glasses, and was shy. He also had friends and rode a motorcycle. Winifred was lonely, with no friends. She still glows when she describes Bernie punching and knocking another guy down the stairs of a dance hall for making a rude comment to her. She told me that this was one of the happiest memories of her life. He fought for her. They were separated by WWII, but she never forgot him. And he never forgot her.

He searched her out years later, after she had produced two children and divorced her husband. I was seven when we met him. I was eight when they married and he moved us out of the city to a small mountain town in Northern California. I remember driving through snow that looked like a Christmas postcard. When we started school, I forgot my new last name and was in big trouble when the school called home to clarify. We were supposed to say that our new Dad was our original dad and our name had always been Paris. I was very excited to finally have a dad and wanted to please him. We were in high school when he formally adopted us. According to my mother, our biological father never responded to the paperwork that was sent back to Kentucky where he lived on a farm with his parents.

Winifred never forgave her mother. Yet, I will always remember the summer day that we were standing in our new neighbor's yard, just down the street from the house we had recently moved into. An unfamiliar car drove slowly by us on the quiet street and my mother seemed to lose her mind. She started chasing it, running down the middle of the street and shouting, "MUD! MUD!" like a barking dog. There were tears streaming down her face as she ran. When the car stopped, I could see that it was my grandmother. We didn't have a phone and she had decided to just drive a few hundred miles to see where we lived.

Mom had begun calling her own mother 'Mud' as a child. The family story was that when Laura returned from one of her long absences, Winifred had followed her around relentlessly, begging for attention, Mother this and Mother that, until Laura shouted in frustration, "I am not 'Mother'. My name is 'MUD!'" This seemed to work for both the abandoner and the abandoned. It stuck. They would both laugh nervously when telling that story and then quickly change the subject.

Winifred has earned a place in the Secret Society of Naked Ladies because, in her 80th decade, she began telling some of her own secrets. She stopped pretending long enough to tell the truth about things she had hidden her entire life. Telling these secrets is not only about having a voice, but also about rebellion. Rebellions can change the world.

She talked about her grandfather raping her and about her grandmother punishing her for telling, and then not protecting her when it continued. She told me about her mother repeatedly abandoning her, and about my biological father who would brutalize her when he drank. She described leaving him, but then he would cry, beg, and promise to change until she came back. According to my mother, my brother was a baby and sleeping in a crib near their bed when his father brought a friend home from the bar. He had run out of money and offered up the "feisty redhead" he had at home in exchange for a few more drinks. When my mother fought back, the baby woke and began crying, and his drunken father threatened to "bash his little head in." He didn't, but I don't know what else happened that night. I do know that she soon packed up and left while he was at work, and then filed for a final divorce. This was long before the Violence Against Women Act was even close to becoming a reality. There was no national hotline and, in those days, what happened between a man and his wife, or a man and his children, was often still considered to be private business. There wasn't even a name for what she experienced back then. There were no Domestic Violence shelters, but she was able to stay with friends-of-friends who he didn't know until she managed to get a place of her own.

According to my grandmother, everyone was sworn to secrecy and Winifred successfully hid from him for months, until the night he showed up at my grandmother's house, drunk, sobbing, and begging her to tell him where his family was. I was an adult when my grandmother covered her face with her hands and admitted to me that she had been the one who told him where her daughter was. She said, "He seemed so sorry." I was conceived that night, after my biological father broke through the door and raped my mother. Again.

I remembered the time when I was in high school that I

snooped through papers and noticed a discrepancy in dates. I questioned Mother about it and instead of being angry, which I expected, she was ready with a story. She told me that she "wanted another baby and had 'tricked him' into making her pregnant after their divorce." Even then, it didn't make sense to me. After my grandmother told me the truth, I understood that my mother didn't want me to feel unwanted. She had been just 24 years old, with limited resources, and already had a baby who was only nine months at the time. Some lies are told with love. They are still lies. It was knowing the truth that allowed me to understand some things I needed to make peace with.

There are people who will surely think I am being treacherous here, but this is my story and I will tell it precisely because it is uncomfortable. Stories like these inform us while secrets do not. I have certainly kept a few of my own. I once told a friend that my mother reported "feeling like she had been given a beautiful gift the day I was born." When I made that up, I helped us both hide. I cannot now imagine her being anything other than exhausted, overwhelmed, and terrified. This is where the real story can be found.

By the time I told you, Randy, the truth about my conception, you knew Winifred and her horrific story. At some point, I mentioned to you that I was thinking about telling her what I knew. You looked quizzically at me and asked how it would help her. I smugly replied that, "The truth is always helpful." You raised your eyebrows and suggested that allowing my elderly mother to believe she has protected me from this information might be the most "generous gift" I could give her. I never told my mother that I knew the truth.

It took tremendous strength for Winifred to break the chain of abuse when her baby boy was threatened. Nobody did that for her when she was a child, and she couldn't do it for herself as a young adult. She protected her children but her scars remained and they sometimes reached for us.

When I was too curious or rebellious, Winifred would tell me that I needed to be "taken down a peg." When she acted on that, she was much less brutal than women in some cultures who hold their young daughters down to have their clitoris cut out. One small example is when the grammar school secretary called to excitedly tell my mother the result of my IQ test. Mom was waiting at the door when I got home and I knew before she spoke that something was wrong. "Those tests don't mean much and they could have made a mistake, so don't be thinking you are SO smart." She ended with, "Your brother doesn't need to hear about this." I had no idea what she was talking about.

Of course, my brother and I both found out and from that day forward, I was routinely called dopey, stupid, rattle-brained, and dingy, along with other similar adjectives some people use to discourage creativity and self confidence in their female children. They never discussed college or what I might be able to contribute or accomplish in life. I still stumble over a lack of self-confidence and anxiety, particularly when someone is expecting a performance from me, like speaking in public. It is a bag of my own internal garbage that I can't seem to dispose of. I kick it down the road, but it is always waiting for me at unexpected times and I must kick it again.

I was slow to find my way into adulthood. My parents paid for my first year at a community college 50 miles away, only because I was barely 17 when I graduated from high school. They were anxious for me, now a rebellious teen, to be gone. My apartment was shared with two other girls and within walking distance to campus. Friends would routinely come there to study between classes. One day my folks dropped by to find the front door open and our friend, Walter, stretched out on the couch with a book. When I got home, he mentioned that my folks had come by and seemed upset, suggesting I call them. Walter was Black.

When I finally reached them, they said that since they found "a big black nigger" laying on my couch, I would not be seeing any more money from them. They didn't know that Walter was also gay. I've often wondered whether knowing that would have subdued or intensified their terror. My landlady informed them that they were responsible for rent through the end of the lease period, adding that they were also legally obligated to support me until I was 18. I had minimal contact with them for several years after that.

Some things are buried deep. I used to believe that when I rejected the concept of racism, I had also exorcized the words and images that were etched into my subconscious. When I was around nine years old, we would often drive past the burned-out shell of a house that sat just off the highway going out of town. It had been there for years, giving haunting and silent testimony to a story I would never fully know. Its blackened roof rafters were caved in and doors gone, while glassless windows offered glimpses of someone's dream that had been demolished. I could see weeds growing through remaining floorboards inside the house and eventually wondered out loud, "What happened to the people who lived there?" My new Dad explained, "They went back to where they belonged! Niggers thought they could live wherever they wanted and got burned out." I was horrified and looked at my mother, thinking she would set her new husband straight. She looked away and never said a word. Even at that young age, I was aware that she had surrendered herself. She became the wife they both believed she needed to be if she was going to be safe. I tried to become the daughter that would please my new dad and began to look away when we drove past that house. It was many years before I looked again and saw it was mostly gone. I began to feel angry with my mother for demonstrating her surrender to me, but then did the same thing in my first marriage. It takes time to weed that carefully planted garden.

It took more years for me to comprehend how deeply racism had burrowed into my psyche. I was 18 and working in San

Francisco when a Black co-worker filed a discrimination lawsuit against the bank we worked for. Along with other white workers, I thought she was a troublemaker. We didn't ask her what her experience had been. I didn't notice that other Black co-workers were silent. Then, there was a friend and co-worker who invited me to her home for dinner and to meet her family. I froze and didn't respond. I remember my mind racing, thinking it wouldn't be safe since most Black men were dangerous. I was afraid. She didn't wait long before turning her back and walking away. We never talked about it.

As a single mom, I developed a friendship with an attractive Black man who wanted a romantic relationship. I couldn't allow myself to explore that. I was afraid of losing what limited support my children and I had. What I did do was repeatedly gather up my kids and leave my parents' house in the middle of a visit, solely because of the hatefully racist things they would say. My parents gradually became quieter about those things when I was around.

A few years before he died, my dad told me that I had made him "think differently about some things." He didn't have to tell me what they were. I remembered the time my daughter, Kristen, and I were visiting when his old friend, Herb, called. They were both nearly deaf so the call was on speaker as they shouted at each other. In response to **"How are you doing?"** Herb yelled that he would be **"doing a lot better when we get that Nigger out of the Whitehouse!"** My dad never even glanced at us and didn't miss a beat before shouting back, **"Well, we probably shouldn't talk about that because we'll just get into a fight."** Kristen and I looked at each other like we had witnessed a miraculous birth. People do change, even in their late 80s and 90s. My mother kept moving in the other direction. She was still afraid.

When Winifred married my dad, she introduced me to open racism. He was also the one who read books, like me. And on summer mornings, he would sit on the porch steps with me and we would whittle pieces of wood with our pocketknives and talk about how some kinds of wood are better for certain things than others; or bet how long the last spot of snow would last on the mountain. He was raised by a raging racist and was also a racist. It took a very long time for me to realize how the words I heard, and the relentless images I saw in print and on TV, had burned into my subconscious mind. When my grandfather led my 12-year-old brother out of the kitchen, saying "Washing dishes is Squaw work" everyone laughed. But it wasn't a joke. He was also brutal to my grandmother. When my dad disgustedly called gospel music "nigger wailing" he was telling us something that had nothing to do with music. I realize while writing this that I never heard my dad sing!

My dad only hit me once, when I was in high school after I told my mother I hated her. When he was home, I usually felt safe. It was dad who taught my brother and I to work hard and take some responsibility. He gave each of us something we would not have had without him.

My brother was not as openly rebellious as me, but instead became cleverly strategic which has served him well. As an adult he has had a successful career and made good money with excellent benefits working for the government. He can be charming and funny, has acquired many friends and just as many secrets. His relationships with women have been predictably complicated. Like Laura Lee and Harold, he and Winifred have remained extremely close and he has served her as the loyal son they both believed he needed to be. No one else could do what he does for his mother.

Now an elderly woman, Winifred has retained a few friends, including several caregivers at her facility who are devoted to her. She has managed to control outbursts of anger with her lovely granddaughters who live out of state and see her only occasionally. This, in turn, has allowed them to make her feel special and loved in ways that she desperately needs.

My mother's relationship with me, the baby she didn't invite, became more difficult as I grew older and less accommodating. Recent studies indicate that severe trauma changes DNA and trauma responses are passed on through generations even when protected from similar trauma. It would have been unbearable for her to examine how her own wounds might have scarred her children and shaped their relationships. As adults, it has become our responsibility to do this, and to change our own harmful behaviors. It is hard work.

Like Winifred and her mother, she and I are deeply connected. She is loved for her strength and for the many beautiful, creative, and humorous things that she also is. My heroes are all flawed.

My most treasured memory of Winifred is of the time that I danced in the rain with her, in a field across from our house. I was 10 or 11 years old when we were walking back home from a neighbor's house and got caught in a summer thunderstorm. Rather than run for cover, she held her arms open and laughed wildly, just like a Naked Lady. She laughed and danced despite lightning that struck too close, and she allowed the rain to wash away all pretense, for a few moments.

It is the woman who danced in the rain that I want never to forget. As she nears the end of her life, I remain close by, even while knowing that danger simmers beneath the scab of the caldron. She is still a sleeping volcano. If I must leave to protect myself from an eruption, we both know that I will be back to sit at my mother's feet.

I could fill many more pages with stories of other Naked Ladies who let us see glimpses of who they really are. That is another book. If I write another book, I might include 'Naked Men'. They would be the men who were strong enough to dismantle the armor of bravado and dominance that hides vulnerable and frightened human beings who have dreams and ambitions that have nothing to do with conquering or controlling anything other than themselves.

A friend recently asked if she could "be in my club" and I had to tell her, "Not until you are demented or dead." I can change names, but if I must ask permission from a live and competent person, I risk being also asked to hold back details that paint a more accurate picture. Even worse, to maintain secrets that hide the source of destructive attitudes and dangerous behaviors.

I like to think that if you were well, we would be discussing, kneeling, donating, and marching together for #MeToo; Black Lives Matter; DACCA; LBGTQ rights; Separation of Church and State; Women's Reproductive rights; and Environmental Justice. We would correct each other if one of us forgets how much the little things we say matter. Each movement is a chorus that raises voices, rather than silencing them, and encourages us to rise together. We don't lose anything when we extend respect, fairness, and opportunity to another.

John Lewis told us that action was as important as praying, and I'm thinking that if we pledge "Liberty and Justice for *all*," we should damn well mean it.

The Bridge to Nowhere

BEFORE AND IMMEDIATELY after your diagnosis, you made your wishes clear. Some, like "Get a gun," or "Throw me off a cliff," weren't a reasonable thing to ask of anyone who loves you. Others were:

1. When I can't feed myself, don't feed me
2. No antibiotics.

I promised. You understood that each would sentence you to a longer life *with dementia*. Antibiotics would not cure your disease or reverse the damage already inflicted. What antibiotics would do is kill the bacteria that might free you. You weren't afraid of death.

We put this in writing, prepared an Advanced Directive, and a POLST. You assigned me Power of Attorney so that I could act on your behalf when you could not. It wasn't enough.

These papers did not educate people about who you were. Papers have not made it easier for some people to elevate your wishes, beliefs, and values above their own. Some caregivers have begun to believe they know you best, and that you enjoy *quality of life* because you often smile and eat the food they bring. Quality of life is a very personal measure. It is one of the reasons we have Advanced Directives and written instructions to speak for us when we can no longer speak for ourselves. Being planted in front of a TV and having food delivered on a schedule might sound like Heaven to some folks. It sounded like Hell to you. You asked not to be taken to Hell even after you became unaware that you were being transported there.

As dementia progresses from one stage to the next, it ebbs and flows like a stream into an ocean that pushes it back during high tide. It is briefly slowed but never stopped from reaching its destination. Like high tide, *end stage dementia* might be pushed back for a while, but it doesn't stop what is coming. End stage assumes that the body is close to dying and sends it to bed, often curled into a fetal position for weeks or months, especially if that body was young and strong when the disease began –– or if it is force-fed and given antibiotics, which interfere with the natural process. End stage introduces complete reliance on busy caregivers to guess whether you feel warm, or cold, terrified, or in pain. In one facility that I visited, I was told that despite antibiotic treatment, most dementia patients eventually die from infection anyway. Others die from choking on their own secretions, or of starvation when they stop accepting food because their bodies and brains no longer have use for it. Sometimes the kindest, most loving, and compassionate thing to do, is *nothing.*

It has been approximately a year and a half since you moved into memory care. You have developed a fever and a cough. At this stage, you are no longer aware of the terminal nature of your illness, or the decisions that are being made on your behalf. You don't remember my promise, but I do.

Pneumonia would be a gift to you. I prepare myself for more conflict because not everyone agrees with your personal choices as outlined in your Advanced Directive.

Your Primary Care Provider (PCP) has finally arrived. He is a soft-bodied, slouching, man who appears to be in his 50s. He is always disheveled, with untidy clothing and hair. Today he has a food stain on the front of his shirt. He rarely makes eye contact because he is always on his way out. He does not want questions, and certainly not a conversation. I was told before you were assigned to him that he has a reputation for not returning phone calls unless they come from the facility nurse who has his private number. I was also told that he relies on this nurse so he doesn't have to show up very often. We have no other choices for PCP because you have become impossible to transport and to manage in waiting rooms, or on exam tables. He is willing to come into the facility to see patients, an important niche to fill. He was rumored to have close to 2,000 patients living in facilities scattered throughout the area, most on Medicaid. This is an unconfirmed rumor that now seems plausible given our experiences.

It is a Friday afternoon, and he is clearly feeling inconvenienced as he impatiently listens to your chest, from the front, through your clothing. He brusquely announces that you have bronchitis, and prescribes Tylenol for fever, and antibiotics for the infection. I remind him of your Advanced Directive and that you did not want antibiotics but only *comfort care*. I also suggest that he listen to your lungs more carefully, as even I could hear deep rails when I laid my ear against your chest. I know that Hospice has requirements for their services and they will make sure you don't suffer. He ignores my request and responds that he will "write a prescription and check back next week," before turning his back and walking out.

Within an hour your fever has risen to 104 degrees and your breathing is more labored. I ask the staff nurse to listen to your lungs from both front *and* back, helping to bend you forward so he can have access. Agreeing that it sounds like pneumonia, he says that one lung seems quite full. I ask him to call Hospice and he refuses, insisting you be given the antibiotics that have already been prescribed. I remind him also that "you did not want any life extending medications." He raises his voice and declares forcefully that **"*Antibiotics are comfort measures and NOT life extending.*"** His authoritative ignorance is as terrifying as ever and I feel my own temperature rising. He first bullies and then pleads with me to allow antibiotics. I repeatedly demand a referral to Hospice, who will relieve your discomfort. He finally declares that he can *read you* and knows what you want. It is very late when he finally surrenders and has the on-call physician make the referral. When Hospice arrives, they confirm the diagnosis and immediately start you on morphine.

I will never forget the relief we both felt as it moves through your system and allows you to relax and sleep. The next day, they have comfort gear and an adjustable bed delivered. I begin sleeping in your recliner, which doesn't stop people from coming in and crying that they don't want you to die.

At the suggestion of a friend, Kathy, who once worked for Hospice, I posted this notice on your door:

ENTER WITH A PEACEFUL HEART

If you are reading this it is because you have been involved in Randy's and my life.

Whether you are family, friend, or caregiver, l know you have loved or deeply cared for Randy, for he is truly one of those people —— that to know him is to love him.

As you all know it has been a challenging road since Randy was diagnosed with FTD a number of years ago.

He and I talked in depth about quality of life and how he wanted things to end, which is reflected in his Advanced Directive. I know that people have different feelings and beliefs about the end of life, but the most important thing to me, and I believe all of you, is helping Randy go out on his own terms.

This is a strenuous, exhausting, and incredibly emotional time for everyone involved. We don't know how long this part of the journey may take and I want and need to focus all my energy on Randy. I need your help to do that.

So, I am asking and hoping that we can all work together in the spirit that is this wonderful person, our Randy Man, to help him fulfill his wishes in the most respectful and dignified way possible.

Appreciatively,
Sandi Paris-Brown

Next, I call close friends, Eric, Martha, and Paula, who drive many miles to support me in protecting you. They circle us both with love. You are still accepting fluids so we know that it could be many days. On the fifth or sixth day, you are peacefully sleeping while we are sitting nearby, telling stories. During a good laugh, I look over at you and see you smile. Then we hear you chuckle, "*Ha ha ha.*" You are feeling better. A day later, there is little doubt that you are on the mend. Your strong body has betrayed you, but I have done my job. Tension in the facility eases over the next few days and things seems to return to normal. I later learn that the staff nurse and your PCP were grumbling to the director and saying in meetings that I had "Tried to kill my husband."

In the meantime, you gradually settle back into the routines of the facility. Months before the pneumonia, I had spent hours cutting and sewing elastic waisted pants and knit shirts together, adding Velcro to close the backs of the shirts which I had cut open. These stopped your increasing tendency to pee on chairs or windows. You had also dropped your pants, twice, and carefully pooped in your recliner before pulling them up and sitting down again. Both of you had to be taken apart and thoroughly cleaned. I bought Dutch Brothers gift cards for front-line staff and got out my sewing machine. These *union-suits* solved the problem nicely and it didn't take long for you to stop trying to remove your clothing. You quickly seemed to forget that you ever had. A side benefit was that you also stopped brazenly scratching your balls. Win-win. After the pneumonia, we agreed that there was no need to reintroduce the union-suits unless you reverted to those behaviors. They were folded and stored in your closet.

During your post-hospice period, we noticed that you began experiencing increased agitation. You were sleeping less and constantly pacing or hovering near the kitchen door for food. When we thought you were dying, Hospice had discontinued all your medications. These calmed you, helped with depression and offset tendencies toward delusions or hallucinations. They were supposed to be titrated back up by your Primary Care Provider and carefully managed for side effects, with dosages requiring adjustment from time to time. I began asking the staff nurse and your PCP to review your medications to be sure they were being brought back to appropriate levels, and to evaluate whether changes were needed. I even provided contact information with a specialist to confer. Each week, I asked the nurse how this was coming along, and each week he would say he had been "too busy." Your agitation increased. One morning he stopped me in the hallway and declared in a booming voice, as if for the benefit of others, "Something has to be done about Randy!" I asked what had happened and he declared, once again, that you were "a danger."

I had a flashback to your first week there, when you had walked out a door that was left open for you. That was the first time he had labeled you "a danger." He also enjoyed words like *aggressive, antagonistic, menacing.* And he seemed preoccupied with behaviors that might be remotely sexual in nature, like scratching your balls.

I was slow to notice the red flag frantically waving in my subconscious mind, trying to get my attention. This person had some power and was planning to use it.

The nurse declined to provide specifics and so I asked as loudly as he, "Why are Randy's medication adjustments not a higher priority, since this is key to managing his behaviors?" I also needed witnesses. This time he promised to "get back to me soon."

The next morning, I received an overly friendly call from him saying that he had "a list of medications ready" and wondered if I could come in while he telephoned our expert at the study center. What a relief! An hour later I walked into an ambush. Management, the Primary Care Provider (PCP), and this staff nurse were waiting to hand me a 10 Day Move-Out notice for you. Rather than a list of medications, he had spent his time creating a list of "dangerous behaviors" that he claimed put you and other residents in jeopardy. He and your PCP had worked together on exaggerated or blatantly untrue accusations that would justify an immediate removal. I was later told they had started hatching this plan after I refused antibiotics on your behalf. *We also discovered that your regular medications had not been properly titrated back up after Hospice terminated care.*

As I scanned through the list of your offenses, it read like something from the Peoples Court in Nazi Germany, which was the original Kangaroo Court. There were no witnesses, no dates or supporting documentation, and the outcome had already been decided. Every single listed offense, whether fabricated or real, was a common behavior in dementia care that had also been observed in other residents at that same facility.

I was utterly speechless before leaving, but eventually advised them that I would be seeking legal advice and then responded:

- Despite being there nearly every day, I have not been made aware of Randy "bruising staff or other residents." Please provide dates, witnesses, Incident Reports, or any documentation related to recent incidents. Also, please explain why I was not notified of this sooner. I am personally aware of at least three incidents where others have assaulted Randy, and he did not retaliate. Are you able to provide a copy and explain your policy on these behaviors?

- Again, I know of just one time, more than a year ago, when he exposed and scratched himself in the TV room. Soon after this, he began wearing uni-suits which stopped that behavior. Why have I not been advised that he *"aggressively exposed himself"* or displayed *"overtly sexual behaviors?"* Please provide dates, witnesses, Incident Reports or any documentation related to these incidents. Perhaps as concerning, can you explain why his uni-suits were not reintroduced to mitigate this new behavior? In addition, I have observed and personally experienced other residents being 'overtly sexual'. Can you explain what your policy is on this very human behavior and how you decide which demented persons might be allowed it, while others are not?

- You stated that the "Behavior Management strategies put in place have been only temporarily successful." Is there any documentation to show how often or how long these strategies were used? Have you also documented the times staff has been too rushed or forgetful to implement them? It was my understanding that they worked well if staff was supported in being consistent. Please provide more specific information as to which strategy worked, how long it worked, and when it stopped working.

- Regarding "taking food from other residents," it is my understanding that this was resolved when it was agreed that he would be given his meal first and in a separate room. I recently stopped by when the caregiver on the floor forgot to do this, yet he remained in the TV room waiting patiently for his meal while others were happily eating in the dining room. Please provide more specific information on why you regarded this as only "temporarily successful."

- "Eating and drinking inappropriate substances" are common dementia behaviors, as are "going in and out of other peoples' rooms." I have personally stopped another resident from drinking fabric softener that was left on the counter. It is also common for other residents to wander in and out of Randy's room and remove his personal belongings. To my knowledge, nobody has been asked to leave because of this behavior. Also, are you aware that modifying the environment to reduce risk is something that most memory care facilities routinely accept as their responsibility?

- Finally, knowing how critical proper medication can be for managing challenging behaviors in dementia patients. Why have you not responded to my repeated requests for a review and adjustment of his medications?

I never minimized the very real and inconvenient challenges that you presented. You are big, strong, and agile, and can be a major inconvenience, but you are not dangerous. I worked to support care staff and most of them love you. In the end. nobody was able to provide documentation or even one example of when you were "aggressive or violent." This language was deliberately inflammatory.

No facility would have accepted you with these things written in your record. I had no choice but to go to battle for you. Again.

It was later confirmed by a concerned staff member that they wanted to evict you in retaliation against me for refusing antibiotics on your behalf. The PCP nurse told people that I "tried to kill my husband." After gathering their own information, the facility manager and owners appeared to realize that they had placed trust in the wrong people. The Move-Out Notice was retracted, and while I do not have access to personnel files, the Director was terminated soon after. The staff nurse lingered with reduced hours and more scrutiny, eventually "retiring." He was rumored to have lost his license. Your PCP was also rumored to have been terminated by the clinic he worked out of and was investigated for Medicaid fraud and allegations of malpractice. I don't know the outcome of those investigations, but another resident's family member told me that they were considering a private lawsuit against both the staff nurse and the same PCP for negligently causing the death and suffering of their mother. Rumors and conjecture cannot be trusted, but after our experience, my personal wish is for these two "professionals" to be housed in a lock-up facility and prevented from ever again accessing vulnerable people who count on compassion above all.

Also troubling, was discovering that the protections put in place by government agencies failed you. These are established to ensure that disabled individuals are safely and reasonably able to access the resources available to them. The day I was given the move-out notice, you were provided with a very nice Ombudsman who informed us of your right to appeal. This person didn't request documentation or question the legitimacy of the action. He did not offer to facilitate an appeal for you. I also learned that the agency responsible for overseeing your services, was notified in phone call by the staff nurse but also did not ask for documentation. Instead, they "trusted" the nurse's claim that you were dangerous and did not ask questions. Nobody contacted me to discuss or prepare us for what was coming, saying they assumed I had been notified and had made plans to move you to some imaginary facility that didn't exist. When I was finally able to speak with someone, she sympathized and then made sure to warn me that if I moved you home, it would be illegal to install locks that would keep you safe.

The levels of failure are gut-wrenching when considering that there are surely other people like yourself, who are not "violent" but have pain-in-the-ass dementia behaviors and might also appear "menacing" because of their flat affect. It's a brain thing. Some may have ended up in psychiatric hospitals and others in jails because nobody else would take them. There are reports of people with FTD trying to survive on the streets before drowning, being beaten, murdered, or suffering other horrific deaths.

Two years after your pneumonia, a staff member was cleaning out resident files when she found a handwritten note in the bottom of yours. It was dated from that time. I was sitting with you in the common room when she walked over and asked if "I had changed my mind and requested antibiotics for you back then?" She knew the story and I laughed because it was ludicrous. "Of course not." She grimly showed me the note that stated, "Randy's wife called to request that he be given the prescribed antibiotics." I was stunned and then outraged. We will never know for sure, but this would explain your miraculous and unexpected recovery from pneumonia.

My first thought was to file a lawsuit. My second thought was to not jeopardize the facility. They have taken many steps to improve quality and consistency of care. I will not take legal action but will share our story here and hope others take away something useful from it. Giving you antibiotics against your wishes made someone else feel righteous and good, while they robbed you of the natural death you had requested. Instead of peace, they sentenced you to more years of decline and confinement. There was nothing ethical or compassionate about this. Antibiotics were a *bridge to nowhere*.

Three years after your pneumonia, many things have changed. Your medications were evaluated and a specialist recommended *Lamictal*, which is commonly used to treat bi-polar symptoms and epilepsy. It has proven to be nothing short of a miracle for you. Within a few days, your overall agitation was reduced. You began to sleep in your bed again and became more peaceful and easier to redirect.

Your disease has now progressed significantly and you no longer appear to recognize the people you love. But you still smile, usually in the mornings. You make no sounds at all and depend entirely on others to keep you clean and comfortable. You are not bedridden and can still walk when encouraged. This usually requires someone to stand in front of you and reach out both hands to grasp yours. We say, "Come on Randy," and pull you up. You happily walk, face to face, to wherever we want you to go.

Under the leadership of the new director and manager, the facility has continued to improve. They devise creative interventions for you and for others. Problems are easier to solve now that staff is more consistently informed and supported. direct-care staff (caregivers) do the hardest and most important work imaginable, at low pay. The facility hired a new, very professional, and compassionate staff nurse, and you have a new Primary Care Provider who is sincerely interested in you. He communicates with me and responds promptly and kindly to your needs as they change.

When you began forgetting to eat, we thought this would be your body's exit strategy. I had promised you that if you "couldn't feed yourself, we would *not* feed you." We switched to finger foods and decided that if you didn't pick them up, we would let it be, which was difficult to do. Both staff and I found ourselves enticing you to take bites. Eventually it was taken out of our hands.

The Advanced Directive form we used allowed you to decline "artificial feeding" which we learned does *not* include spoon-feeding. In recent years, a family in Ashland, Oregon sued a local care facility to stop spoon-feeding their wife and mother who had specified this in her own Advanced Directive. The facility insisted on feeding her for as long as she accepted and swallowed the food, even though it contradicted her wishes. If they had not interfered, she would likely have died a natural death within a matter of weeks. I heard that the Ombudsmen organization intervened on behalf of the woman, against her family. The court ruled that the facility was indeed obligated to continue spoon-feeding her for as long as she "accepted and swallowed" the food. She lived many months more. What the rule makers seem unable to consider is that many people like you, with advanced dementia, will reflexively open their mouths and chew on whatever touches their lips... a finger, paper clip, hearing aids, someone's cigarette, artificial flower, or electrical cord... and sometimes swallow them. Until there is another legal challenge to this, it is out of my control.

Those of us who know and love you are hoping for another pneumonia. I am confident that your wish to avoid treatments that extend your life will now be honored, except for being *hand-fed*. A medical person explained to me, "It looks bad when people starve to death in a care facility." In reality, death from starvation is common. When the brain stops recognizing food, it can be a relatively pain-free exit and spare someone many months of unnecessary confinement and suffering. It appears that you will most likely avoid end-stage dementia only if you have a massive stroke, fatal heart attack, or acquire another serious infection. If the latter happens, we can give you morphine, which makes you smile in your sleep even when you are very sick. *I want that for you.*

In the meantime, you still hold my hand and listen to my voice. You smile and breathe in and out, again and again. I sometimes forget that one day, no matter what we do or don't do, this will stop.

It has now been six days since they found you chewing on a blanket that was soaked in blood from your infected gums. We have been unable to clean your mouth for over two years.

You are running a fever and have stopped accepting food. We believe that bacteria from your mouth have entered your bloodstream. This time I do not have to go into warrior mode. You have a team of caring professionals who will honor your wishes. They will comfort you and make sure that no one slips you antibiotics.

Hospice thinks it will be a week or more. You are increasingly uncomfortable and at my request they increase your morphine to the maximum dose. They will be back tomorrow to check on you. I stay with you until after midnight. Staff promises to call if anything changes, and I go home to sleep. After just a few hours, I wake up and can't fall back to sleep.

When I arrive back at your facility, a dear caregiver named Sarah tells me that you have been very uncomfortable and restless most of the time I was gone. She has been sitting and reading to you, just so you could hear a voice. When she leaves, your eyes follow her and then rest on me. I kiss your cheek and take your hand, lacing my fingers with yours. Your breathing seems erratic so I begin to count the spaces in between. It gives me something to do. You have been writhing with pain off and on over the past three days. The morphine works for just an hour or two and then you become increasingly uncomfortable until the next scheduled dose. It later turns out that there was a miscommunication between Hospice and the med-tech who doesn't understand that *the same dose can be given more frequently, as needed.* Now, when caregivers come in and roll you over, you cry out in pain, "Ahhhh!" I haven't heard your voice for more than a year and this sound tortures me. When they leave, you calm, and your eyes search my face. I stroke your head, whispering my mantra, "You are the best man I know." I tell you how happy you have made me. You begin to pant, quick little breaths that remind me of when I gave birth to my children. Even so, I don't realize what is happening.

I get up and turn on your iPod and Don Henley's voice

randomly fills the room to softly sing "Goodbye to a River." This song had special meaning and you become very still, listening. You watch my face closely when I sing along, like we used to do together. I sit on your bed and take your hand again, holding it against my cheek. Your eyes are on mine, but after a while they stop focusing on me. I can't follow this gaze. As the song ends, your fingers let go as if on cue. I squeeze your hand, but you don't squeeze back. You exhale and I do, too. I begin to count again. One, two, three... after 20 counts, you start to take another breath, but then you don't. You just stop. I keep gripping your hand and holding my own breath until my body rebels and insists that I suck in air. I gasp and choke on tears. I lay my head on your chest, feeling your warmth. There is no heartbeat. No drummer to lead. I stay like that for a long time. If any part of you is still here, I want you to know that I am too. Once again, I am unprepared.

I don't know how long I have been sitting here. Some people believe the soul hovers over the body for hours or even days, after death. You didn't believe in a soul. You also didn't believe that we know everything. At some point, your body felt empty to me. I don't know if it was because you left or because I accepted that you were gone. I don't weep because I want to keep you here like this. Tears flow because I can't know what you were feeling and I can't see where you have gone. I am shattered by your unexpected suffering and I cry with relief that it is ended. I also cry because I don't know what I am going to do now.

When I raise my head, I look at my watch and note that it is 9 AM. Exactly. I know that people will ask for *the time* even though it has probably been more than 20 minutes since you stopped breathing. You would approve of my being late. I walk out to tell staff, and then come back to sit with you and look at your face one last time. It is still beautiful. I brush back your dark hair, and trace my fingers across your forehead, along your angular nose, over your graying mustache and down over your lips. I gently try to close your eyelids, like they do in the movies, but they won't stay closed. Another myth exposed.

As I sit with you these final moments, I begin to imagine your sweet and playful energy scattering like glitter being blown by an unexpected breeze. You are everywhere while I am still here, without you.

People are coming in and I know it is time to go. The Hospice Social Worker drives me home but I don't remember the ride. I remember kissing your forehead and whispering, "Later Gator." I don't want to talk but will need to very soon. I must quickly make arrangements for your brain to be removed and transported on dry ice to the Memory and Aging Center so it can be autopsied. You were a scientist, and this is what you wanted.

Epilogue

Putting these experiences and memories back into words has moved them outside of myself, allowing us both to complete a journey. Words have met their purpose of carrying thoughts and stories into other minds and hearts. They have given me back what I lost when Randy forgot my stories. I am not alone.

It has been six months since Randy's death and time feels different now. It is not faster or slower, but somehow more generous. Each morning when I awake, I am surprised to find the luxurious gift of time placed gently in my lap – like a prepaid ticket. If I were to flick my tongue and taste the air, it would taste like freedom lingering for a moment. I savor it like my first sip of coffee laced with heavy cream and allow it to lead me into my day. Sometimes, I roll over and go back to sleep.

The house doesn't feel lonely but bursts with energy, memories, photos, books, and flowers. It is cozy with color and light, and noisy with music that I play whenever I want. Some evenings I drink wine all by myself, dance in the kitchen, or play Leonard Cohen and cry. Other times I call old friends and we share a bonding rant of political outrage and laughter. Mostly I work in the garden, listen to the birds and smile. At this very moment, I have opened the window next to my desk and am chuckling at the baby tree swallows in the birdhouse. They have grown so big that there is almost no room for the parents to tend them. They are as noisy and demanding as teenagers preparing to leave for college. It is time to get out there and take some risks – time to fly.

Covid-19 has reminded me again how unpredictable life is. It has given me permission to write, garden, cook, and walk each day. I avoid crowds, yet my body and mind continue to take me to interesting places. People I love still show me who I am, whether I like it or not. Video chats with grandchildren is always startling when I see my aging face in the reverse camera. The Crone has emerged but she is still taking risks. Telling secrets to strangers is a big one. I strive for dignity and grace, but still say, "fuck" too much. An unnecessary rebellion that just feels good.

Facing conflict, speaking up for those without a voice, and standing against injustice are small, sporadic achievements. Surrendering to love has been the single most courageous thing I have done. It is by far the most dangerous.

Each time I succumb to the joyful terror of loving another person, I must forget that one day I will have my heart ripped from my chest while it is still beating. This is the price I have been willing to pay for moments of exquisite joy and intimacy with another living being. The richest and most interesting people I have met, do this willingly, over and over, for children, lovers, family, friends, even pets. There is nothing more intoxicating than stepping into its familiar current to be transported to places unknown.

Tim Zandee

★ ★ ★ ★

Randy Brown

Randy died on February 18th, 2020, at the age of 61, just before Covid-19 closed his facility to visitors. I am grateful that I was able to be with him during his final moments. I can only imagine how agonizing it is for people who are now prevented from doing this. His obituary describes him riding his bicycle through the universe with arms held up in victory. It is how I envision him now, joyously free of FTD and riding where he can't get lost or have a flat tire. Sometimes I laugh and talk out loud to him, just like Mary talked to George. He is not under a gravestone, but in a wooden box that sits on the table under my bedroom window where I watch yellow finches flitting about like little promises wrapped in gold. Ashes will scatter one day, but for now I am still holding on.

★ ★ ★ ★

Winifred Paris

Winifred stopped fighting in May of 2019 at the age of 97. She finally allowed Hospice to ease her pain and two of her beautiful granddaughters, Becky, and Betsy, were able to join our vigil and sit with her, paint her fingernails, and tell her she was loved. Caregivers and other staff frequently stopped in, and we all took turns making sure that she had someone with her, caressing and loving her during every moment of her final hours. *It is all she ever wanted.* A couple of weeks before she died, she told me she was "sorry". She didn't say what for and I didn't ask, but just patted her hand. I had never heard that word pass her lips. Not once. And I liked the idea of putting it wherever I needed it to be, like a healing salve. I gently replied, "Everything is OK, Mom." She nodded and looked toward the window, perhaps at the plant that looked dry. Mom's ashes were mixed with Dad's and scattered together in an ancient redwood grove that they loved to visit. As I held her hands during those last days, I noticed how spotted and wrinkled they were – just like Laura Lee's in the retirement photo that shows her holding onto the big steering wheel she was preparing to let go of. My hands are their hands. Their trauma is my trauma. The healing that comes with their release belongs to us all.

★ ★ ★ ★

Gus-Gus

Sweet Gus-Gus left us in 2018. He was my constant companion and entertainer during our journey through dementia. At 13 he began having recurrent intestinal pain, diarrhea and vomiting. After tests indicated pancreatic and liver tumors, the veterinarian gently suggested that I relieve his suffering. I held him close and stroked him while he drifted away. I am convinced that he never once questioned whether life was worth living. I imagine him at the beach gleefully chasing waves and then frantically running when they chase him back. I miss him every day.

★ ★ ★ ★

Patricia Brown

Patricia Brown passed on October 20, 2015. She was always terrified of being "put into a *Home*," and her lovely daughter, Terri, was able to keep her with them to the end. Before she moved to Texas, the memory of her degrees and professional years of nursing had faded, but she could still express pride in not being a 'Divorcee.' While legally separated for years, her husband died before she did and if she had been able, I believe she would have claimed *Widow* with equal pride. Some of Pat's ashes were scattered in Mexico where my friends, Tom and Margie, drove me to find remote cave paintings that Pat had wanted to visit. Terri has scattered some in Hawaii where she also hoped to go one day. The remainder have been placed in Ohio near her *Mommy* and *Daddy*. She is back home.

★ ★ ★ ★

Scott Mathis

Scott now lives very nearby, here in Southern Oregon. It became too precarious for me to travel mountain passes for the emergencies that began happening more frequently. At 53 he has some wrinkles and threads of grey in his hair. He doesn't like you to mention these. More than a year ago, he had a minor stroke, which precipitated his move to Oregon. Recovered fully, he still plays a merciless game of checkers and has adjusted beautifully to his new home. If I leave this earth before he does, he will be safe and cared for by his new foster family. Scott is also beginning to experience some cognitive decline but will smile and tell you he is "just fine" when asked.

When I told Scott that Randy had died, I reminded him we would always be able to visit him in the photographs and memories we have. He was somber as he nodded his head. I asked if he remembered what Randy was like "before his brain got sick." He studied my face and then said, "Yes, I do." I asked what he remembered, and after a very, very, long pause, he said, "Frogs." I responded, *"Erreet, Erreet"* and we both giggled. He is better than just fine.

Afterword

From the moment we began searching for a diagnosis, I leapt from one resource to another. First seeking useful information and then attempting to access compassionate *person-centered* care. This is the standard of care that most professionals, agencies, and facilities strive for, but struggle to deliver.

In our case, no one in our rural area was prepared to accommodate a tall, strong, man in his 50s who exhibited typical dementia behaviors. Jail is not an appropriate alternative.

Like navigating wobbly stones across a raging river, I was grateful that each resource was in place, but never sure if it would lead to safety or toss us back into a current of fear and uncertainty.

Our personal stories may contribute to identifying solutions and strategies that might be explored as we face the tsunami of dementia that is expected to challenge our health care systems soon. We are not ready.

According to an updated Fact Sheet from the Alzheimer's Association: (Alz.org):

- FTD accounts for approximately 10% of all dementias. This may be a low count since many are misdiagnosed. It remains the most common of young dementias, striking between the ages of 40 and 65. An uncommon age for any dementia, it can devastate young families.
- 5.8 million (1 in 10 over age 65) Americans currently live with a Dementia. This number is expected to double by 2050.
- In 2020, dementia care cost the nation an estimated $305 billion
- By 2050, dementia care will cost the nation an estimated $1.1 trillion (in 2020 dollars)

- As our elder population rapidly increases, so will the number of dementias that require care. It is a leading cause of extended disability.
- Dementia predominantly impacts ethnic minorities and women, who also absorb most of the burden for caregiving. We need to understand why if we are to find solutions.
- There is an urgent need to develop more rational, respectful, and compassionate responses to end-of-life choices.

The medical systems and programs in place to assist Randy have faltered but did not entirely fail him because of constant vigilance and repeated advocacy. Some individuals in positions of power were unwilling to honor his wishes for compassionate end-of life care. However, other individuals within these same systems, stepped up to join us in advocating for solutions. Groups of individuals with shared vision and determination will, as always, drive change.

The question that continues to haunt me is this: ***What happens to those who have no warrior of their own?***

Resources

- **The Association for Frontotemporal Degeneration** at www.theaftd.org is a wonderful organization that offers extensive information and assistance specific to FTD type dementias. They estimate that there are currently around 60,000 cases of FTD in the United States.
- **The Alzheimer's Association** at www.alz.org provides valuable information on numerous kinds of dementias, not just Alzheimer's.
- **Hospice Foundation of America**: https://www.hospicefoundation.org
- **Elder Law Answers**: https://www.elderlawanswers.com
- **Advanced Directive specific to dementia.** Death with Dignity: https://www.deathwithdignity.org/alzheimers-dementia-directive/
- **National Down Syndrome Society**: NDSS.org. (What is Down syndrome?)
- **National Alliance to End Homelessness**: https://endhomelessness.org/homelessness-in-america
- **Universal Child Care**: Lanham Act Universal Child Care: https://obamawhitehouse.archives.gov/blog/2015/01/22/experiment-universal-child-care-united-states-lessons-lanham-act
- **Domestic Violence**: Information at www.thehotline.org. Call 800-799-7233.

RECOMMENDED READING

- *A Three Dog Night*, a memoir, by Abigail Thomas; published in the United States by Harcourt Publishing, 2006. (I keep Thomas's book on my nightstand for when I need company in the night.)
- *Educated*, a memoir, by Tara Westover; published in the United States by Random House, 2018. (Westover's book stays at the top of my stack so I can find it quickly when I want to be inspired by her courage in reaching for knowledge and freedom at such a young age and under her circumstances. It took me many more years.)
- *My Heart Can't Even Believe It*, a story of science, love, and Down syndrome, by Amy Silverman; published in the United States, by Woodbine House, 2016. (Always brilliant and funny, here Silverman is also honest, informative, and full of love).
- *Between The World and Me*, by Ta-Nehisi Coates; published in Australia by The Text Publishing Company, 2015. (Coates writes to his adolescent son about the danger of inhabiting a black body in the United States. He notes that the earth is also being treated with a similarly violent disregard, by humans who dream the same destructive dream, that they are white. I find myself remembering how female bodies have also been exploited, demeaned, subjugated, and physically abused for centuries. Racism and misogyny are separate arms of the same monster. Coates makes me want to shut-up and listen.)
- *Men Who Hate Women*, by Laura Bates; Published in Great Britain by Simon & Schuster UK Ltd, 2020. (Bates passionate analysis of modern misogyny is as important to me as Ta-Nehisi Coates examples of systemic racism. For any human who is confused about what sexism and

misogyny looks like and how it affects us all, Bates is a place to start. I am deeply grateful for this book.)

- *Untamed; This is how you find yourself*, by Glennon Doyle; Published in the United States by Random House, 2020. (Doyle is so fast and brilliant, I want her to live next door. She is one of several amazing young women who tell us how to be brave and vulnerable, but she breaks it down so that it is immediately useful. Even at my age I feel a little wilder after reading Doyle. When I begin to question whether I might be too old to be a "writer," I hear her voice reminding me to answer, "I *am* a writer!" I am.)

- *Wild, by Cheryl Strayed*; published in the United States by Knophf Borzoi Books, a division of Random House, 2020. (I absolutely love Strayed! Her epic openness hurts and then heals; embarrasses and then shines with pride and forgiveness. She reminds me to keep moving.)

- *Rising Strong: How the Ability to Reset Transforms the Way We Live, Love, Parent, and Lead;* by Brene' Brown; Published in the United States in 2017, by Random House. (Brown wasn't around 40 years ago, but I love her like one of my smart and fearless friends who *know what I know*, only with more depth and precision; and who *think like I think*, but more quickly and clearly. If you don't have time to read anything else, read Brene' Brown! She will happily cut through the bullshit for you and kick shame to the curb. She places the crown of courage on top of vulnerability, which makes all things possible. I pop this book open when I want to read the words of a smart and funny woman who uses everyday language, including profanity, and doesn't apologize for being human.

- *What my Bones Know: A Memoir of Healing from Complex Trauma;* by Stephanie Foo. Published in 2022 by Ballantine Books. (Foo pulls fascinating research together while sharing her personal stories of trauma, and how it moves through our bodies, alters our DNA, and changes our lives in ways we often don't recognize. Foo validates what I know about my mother and grandmothers, and how their trauma also affected their children. I have not finished this book but want it on the list because it is already important to me.)

Acknowledgments

It would take 100's of pages to properly thank every person who has enriched my life and Randy's. Those who contributed the most to my sanity and to the creation of this unapologetically honest and somewhat controversial book are here.

Ardeth and Dave: Thank you for bringing Randy and I together and walking through his illness with us. Your steady friendship over the decades, and your unwavering support for the book is one of the reasons it exists.

Margie: For your readings and for always knowing when to show up and what to do. Your tenacity and love have carried Randy, Gus, and me when everyone else was damn tired. Your confidence and enthusiasm for the book have pushed me forward once again.

Candy: For your love and loyalty. My constant friend who never really left, we grew together, saw each other through divorces and raising kids. You loved Scott like one of your own. You are family and I always know that you are there, somewhere, ready to spring into action for a little work or fun.

Eric: For your thorough & repeated early reading and input. You have filled so many places in my heart, my garden, and my moving truck. Thank you for also being there for Randy, and for the walking phone calls that feed my ranting soul.

Martha & Eric; Candy and Kent; Tom and Margie: You are my dream teams! You have showed up countless times for Randy and for me. Thank you for your help and encouragement over the years and for staying in my life no matter what. I love each of you, together and apart.

SPATs - Anne Holcomb, Pam Brown, and Tamar Danufsky: Thank you for reading and for the years of great food, wine, tears, and laughter. Your brilliance and kindness continue to sustain me. May we have many more waitresses and bartenders running out the door for hugs before we leave.

Pam Tuson: For early reading and help with packing, gardening, and paving. Your thoughtful generosity and sharing of grief through transition meant more than you know. There is nothing you can't do.

Paula: I will never forget your courage and honesty, and for traveling to hold vigil with Eric, Martha, and I, the first time Randy was dying. I am eternally grateful that your loyalty to Randy extended to me.

Roxanna, Martha, Ruthie, Connie, Sam, and **Jordi:** I am grateful for your early reading and sweet friendship. The gift of your precious time and insight on these stories was invaluable.

Raeanne Bossarte: Special thanks to you, my dear friend, for stepping in at the last moment to read and expertly cut much, but not all, of my written rants. Yours is another loyal and enduring friendship over many years.

My children:

Kari Bear: I will always remember your heroic efforts in keeping Randy safe and distracted on that wild ride through town. You are persevering, kind, and generous, and make the world a better place.

JB Brown: Thank you for putting your life aside and supporting us when we needed you. Your Dad loved *you* more than anyone in the world and he would be so very proud of the man you have become.

Kristen Marie: Thank you for the daily phone calls, thoughtful gifts, advice, and laughter. You always surprise and inspire me, and your visits are like rain on my always thirsty soul.

Scooter: Thanks for being our precious "goofball." You never let us forget what is important.

I am honored to watch each of you courageously navigate your very different lives. I am proud to know you.

To Randy's and my own extended family: I am aware that these intimate stories might impact each of you in unexpected ways. I want to honor Randy's sisters and their families, as well as my brother and his family. You have also sacrificed and I am eternally grateful that you have been part of our lives. I recognize that you have your own stories to tell.

Additional gratitude goes to the many other people who also helped keep Randy engaged and out of jail, and who gave me respite. I am deeply touched by those who allowed themselves to be uncomfortable, even fondled. You opened your hearts to Randy as his behaviors became increasingly unpredictable and never told me that I should stop crying, even when I wanted to. You kept us from being isolated. ***You know who you are!***

Thanks also to Kona Morris and Robert McDowell for editorial efforts and literary feedback.